Guide to Homeopathy

ALTERNATIVE · THERAPIES ·

GEDDES&
GROSSET

WARNING

No course of treatment should be undertaken without the advice of your doctor.

Do not take homeopathic remedies without supervision by a trained homeopathic practitioner.

You should never stop taking or reduce any medication without the approval of your doctor.

This edition published 2007 by Geddes & Grosset

David Dale House, New Lanark, ML11 9DJ, Scotland

First published 1996
Reprinted 1999 (twice), 2007

Cover photograph by Rita Maas, courtesy of the Image Bank

ISBN 978 1 85534 229 3

Printed and bound in India

Contents

Introduction

The aim of homeopathy is to cure an illness or disorder by treating the whole person rather than merely concentrating on a set of symptoms. Hence, in homeopathy the approach is holistic, and the overall state of health of the patient, especially his or her emotional and psychological wellbeing, is regarded as being significant. A homeopath notes the symptoms that the person wishes to have cured but also takes time to discover other signs or indications of disorder that the patient may regard as being less important. The reasoning behind this is that illness is a sign of disorder or imbalance within the body. It is believed that the whole 'make-up' of a person determines, to a great extent, the type of disorders to which that individual is prone and the symptoms likely to occur. A homeopathic remedy must be suitable both for the symptoms and the characteristics and temperament of the patient. Hence, two patients with the same illness may be offered different remedies according to their individual natures. One remedy may also be used to treat different groups of symptoms or ailments.

Homeopathic remedies are based on the concept that

'like cures like', an ancient philosophy that can be traced back to the 5th century BC, when it was formulated by Hippocrates. In the early 1800s, this idea awakened the interest of a German doctor, Samuel Hahnemann, who believed that the medical practices at the time were too harsh and tended to hinder rather than aid healing. Hahnemann observed that a treatment for malaria, based on an extract of cinchona bark (quinine), actually produced symptoms of this disease when taken in a small dose by a healthy person. Further extensive studies convinced him that the production of symptoms was the body's way of combating illness. Hence, to give a minute dose of a substance that stimulated the symptoms of an illness in a healthy person could be used to fight that illness in someone who was sick. Hahnemann conducted numerous trials (called 'provings'), giving minute doses of substances to healthy people and recording the symptoms produced. Eventually, these very dilute remedies were given to people with illnesses, often with encouraging results.

Modern homeopathy is based on the work of Hahnemann, and the medicines derived from plant, mineral and animal sources are used in extremely dilute amounts. Indeed, it is believed that the curative properties are enhanced by each dilution because impurities that might cause unwanted side effects are lost. Substances used in homeopathy are first soaked in alcohol to extract their essential ingredients. This initial solution, called the 'mother tincture', is diluted successively either by factors of ten (called the 'decimal scale' and designated X) or 100 (the 'centesimal scale' and designated C). Each dilution is shaken vigorously before further ones are made, and this is thought to make the properties more powerful by adding energy at each stage while impurities are removed. The thorough shakings of each dilution are said to energise, or 'potentiate', the medicine. The remedies are made into tablets or may be used in the form of ointment, solutions, powders, suppositories, etc. High potency (i.e. more dilute) remedies are used for severe symptoms and lower potency (less dilute) for milder ones.

The homeopathic view is that during the process of healing, symptoms are redirected from more important to less important body systems. It is also held that healing is from innermost to outermost parts of the body and that more recent symptoms disappear first, this being known as the 'law of direction of cure'. Occasionally, symptoms may worsen initially when a homeopathic remedy is taken, but this is usually short-lived and is known as a 'healing crisis'. It is taken to indicate a change and that improvement is likely to follow. Usually, with a homeopathic remedy, an improvement is noticed fairly quickly although this depends upon the nature of the ailment, health, age and well-being of the patient and potency of the remedy.

A first homeopathic consultation is likely to last about one hour so that the specialist can obtain a full picture of the patient's medical history and personal circumstances. On the basis of this information, the homeopathic doctor decides on an appropriate remedy and potency (which is usually 6C). Subsequent consultations are generally shorter, and full advice is given on how to store and take the medicine. It is widely accepted that homeopathic remedies are safe and non-addictive, but they are covered by the legal requirements governing all medicines and should be obtained from a recognised source.

Potency table for homeopathic medicines

The centesimal scale		
1C =	1/100 ($1/100^{1}$)	of mother tincture
2C =	1/10 000 ($1/100^{2}$)	of mother tincture
3C =	1/1 000 000 ($1/100^{3}$)	of mother tincture
6C =	1/1 000 000 000 000 ($1/100^{6}$)	of mother tincture
The decimal scale		
1X =	1/10 ($1/10^{1}$)	of mother tincture
2X =	1/100 ($1/10^{2}$)	of mother tincture
6X =	1/1 000 000 ($1/10^{6}$)	of mother tincture

The development of homeopathy

The Greek physician Hippocrates, who lived several hundred years before the birth of Christ (460–370 BC), is regarded as the founding father of all medicine. The Hippocratic Oath taken by newly qualified doctors in orthodox medicine binds them to an ethical code of medical practice in honour of Hippocrates. Hippocrates believed that disease resulted from natural elements in the world in which people lived. This contrasted with the view that held sway for centuries that disease was some form of punishment from the gods or God. He believed that it was essential to observe and take account of the course and progress of a disease in each individual, and that any cure should encourage that person's own innate healing power. Hippocrates embraced the idea of 'like being able to cure like' and had many remedies that were based on this principle. Hence, in his practice and study of medicine he laid the foundations of the homeopathic approach although this was not to be appreciated and developed for many centuries.

During the period of Roman civilisation a greater knowledge and insight into the nature of the human body was developed. Many herbs and plants were used for healing by people throughout the world, and much knowledge was gained and handed down from generation to generation. The belief persisted, however, that diseases were caused by supernatural or divine forces. It was not until the early 1500s that a Swiss doctor, Paracelsus (1493–1541), put forward the view that disease resulted from external environmental forces. He also believed that plants and natural substances held the key to healing and embraced the 'like can cure like' principle. One of his ideas, known as the 'doctrine of signatures', was that the appearance of a plant, or the substances it contained, gave an idea of the disorders it could cure.

In the succeeding centuries, increased knowledge was gained about the healing properties of plants and the way the human body worked. In spite of this, the methods of medical practice were extremely harsh, and there is no doubt that many people suffered needlessly and died because of the treatment they received. It was against this background that Samuel Hahnemann (1755–1843), the founding father of modern homeopathy, began his work as a doctor in the late 1700s. In his early writings, Hahnemann criticised the severe practices of medicine and advocated a healthy diet, clean living conditions and high standards of hygiene as a means of improving health and warding off disease. In 1790, he became interested in quinine, extracted from the bark of the cinchona tree, which was known to be an effective treatment for malaria. He tested the substance first on himself, and later on friends and close family members, and recorded the results. These early experiments were called 'provings'. The results led him to conduct many further investigations and provings of other natural substances, during the course of which he rediscovered and established the principle of like being able to cure like.

By 1812, the principle and practice of homeopathy, based on the work of Hahnemann, had become established, and many other doctors adopted the homeopathic approach. Hahnemann himself became a teacher in homeopathy at the University of Leipzig and published many important writings – the results of his years of research. He continued to practise, teach and conduct research throughout his life, especially in producing more dilute remedies that were succussed, or shaken, at each stage and were found to be more potent. Although his work was not without its detractors, Hahnemann had attracted a considerable following by the 1830s. In 1831 there was a widespread cholera epidemic in central Europe for which Hahnemann recommended treatment with camphor. Many people were cured, including Dr Frederick Quin (1799–1878), a medical practitioner at that time. He went on to establish the first homeopathic hospital in London in 1849. A later resurgence of cholera in Britain enabled the effectiveness of camphor to be established beyond doubt, as the numbers of people cured at the homeopathic hospital were far greater than those treated at other hospitals.

In the United States of America, homeopathy became firmly established in the early part of the 19th century, and there were several eminent practitioners who further enhanced knowledge and practice. These included Dr Constantine

Hering (1800–80), who formulated the 'laws of cure', explaining how symptoms affect organ systems and move from one part of the body to another as a cure occurs. Dr James Tyler Kent (1849–1916) introduced the idea of constitutional types, which is now the basis of classical homeopathy, and advocated the use of high potency remedies.

In the later years of the 19th century, a fundamental split occurred in the practice of homeopathy, which was brought about by Dr Richard Hughes (1836–1902), who worked in London and Brighton. He insisted that physical symptoms and the nature of the disease itself was the important factor rather than the holistic approach based on the make-up of the whole individual person. Hughes rejected the concept of constitutional types and advocated the use of low potency remedies. Although he worked as a homeopath, his approach was to attempt to make homeopathy more scientific and to bring it closer to the practices of conventional medicine. Some other homeopathic doctors followed the approach of Hughes, and the split led to a collapse in faith in the whole practice of homeopathy during the earlier part of the 20th century. As the 20th century advanced, however, homeopathy regained its following and respect. Conventional medicine and homeopathy have continued to advance, and there is now a greater sympathy and understanding between the practitioners in both these important disciplines.

Homeopathic Remedies in Common Use

Aconitum napellus

Aconite, monkshood, wolfsbane, friar's cap, mousebane

Aconitum is a native plant of Switzerland and other mountainous regions of Europe, where it grows in the damp conditions of alpine meadows. Attractive purple/dark blue flowers are borne on tall, upright stems produced from tubers developed from the root system. Aconite is highly poisonous, and its sap was used by ancient hunters on the ends of their arrows. 'Wolfsbane' refers to this use, and *Aconitum* is derived from the Latin word *acon*, meaning 'dart'. This was one of the homeopathic remedies extensively tested and proved by Hahnemann. He used it for the acute infections and fevers, accompanied by severe pain, that were usually treated by blood-letting by the physicians of his day. This remains its main use in modern homeopathy, and the whole plant is used to produce the remedy.

Aconite is a valuable treatment for acute illnesses of rapid onset in people who have previously been healthy and well.

Aconitum napellus

These often occur after the person has been out in cold wet weather. It is used especially at the start of feverish respiratory infections, such as colds and influenza and those affecting the eyes and ears. The person usually experiences restlessness, a hot, flushed face, muscular pains and disturbed sleep but may be pale when first getting up. It is also used to treat the menopausal symptoms of hot flushes. It is an effective remedy for some mental symptoms, including extreme anxiety and fear, palpitations and attacks of panic, especially the belief that death is imminent during illness. The remedy encourages sweating and is sometimes used in conjunction with BELLADONNA. Symptoms are made worse by cold, draughts, tobacco smoke, stuffy, airless, warm rooms, listening to music at midnight and by lying on the painful part. They improve out in the fresh air and with warmth. The people who benefit from Aconite are typically strong, solid or well-built, high-coloured and usually enjoy good health but have a poor opinion of themselves. Because of this, they tend to have a constant need to prove their own worth, to the point of insensitivity or unkindness to others. When in good health, Aconite people have a need for the company of others. However, they also have fears that they keep concealed and may be frightened of going out or of being in a crowd. When ill, they are inclined to be morbid and to believe that death is imminent, and they cope badly with any kind of shock.

Actea racemosa

Actea rac.; cimic,, *Cimifuga racemosa*, black snakeroot, rattleroot, bugbane, rattleweed, squawroot.

This plant is a native of woodlands in North America and was used by the American Indian peoples as a remedy for the bite of the rattlesnake. It was also used as a tranquilliser and for pain relief in labour and menstruation. An infusion made from the plant was sprinkled in the home to protect against supernatural forces and evil spirits. The plant has a dark, woody underground stem (rhizome) and roots, and produces feathery, tall stems of white flowers. The fresh rhizomes and roots are used in homeopathy, being collected, cut and dried in the autumn after the stems and leaves have died down and the fruit has been formed. The rhizome has a faint, unpleasant smell and the taste is acrid and bitter. The remedy was extensively tested and proved by the English homeopath Dr Richard Hughes, who used it in the treatment of a stiff neck and associated headache. It is used for this purpose in modern homeopathy and also to treat pain in the lower back and between the shoulder blades. Also for rheumatic pain and swelling of joints or muscles and other sudden, sharp pains. Actea rac. is considered to be of great value in the treatment of menstrual problems with cramps, bloatedness, and pain and symptoms of pregnancy, e.g. morning sickness and abdominal discomfort. It is also of value for postnatal depression and menopausal symptoms. Emotional symptoms that accompany these periods of hormonal change, such as weepiness, anxiety and irritability, are also eased by this remedy. Symptoms are made worse by exposure to cold, wet, draughty conditions, by any sudden change in the weather, on drinking alcohol and with excitement. They improve with keeping warm, with gentle exercise and in the fresh, open air. A person suitable for this remedy is often a woman. She may be a bubbly, extrovert, talkative person or withdrawn, depressed and sad, heaving great sighs. The woman is usually emotionally intense with a fear of dying and madness. These fears are at their height in a woman going through the menopause.

Allium

Allium cepa; Spanish onion

The onion has been cultivated and used for many centuries, both for culinary and medicinal purposes, and was important in the ancient Egyptian civilisation. The volatile oil released when an onion is sliced stimulates the tear glands of the eyes and mucous membranes of the nose, throat and air passages. Hence, in homeopathy the onion is used to treat ailments with symptoms of a streaming nose and watering eyes. The red Spanish onion, which is cultivated throughout the world, is used to make the homeopathic remedy. It is used to treat allergic conditions, such as hay fever, colds and pains or symptoms that go from one side to the other. It is useful for shooting, stabbing or burning pains associated with neuralgia, which may alternate from side to side, frontal headaches, painful molar teeth and is also effective in treating earache in children. The symptoms are made worse by cold, damp conditions and improve in fresh air and cool, dry surroundings.

Apis mellifica

Apis; *Apis mellifera*, the honey bee

The source of the medicine is the entire body of the honey bee, which is crushed or ground to prepare the remedy. It is used particularly to treat inflammation, redness, swelling and itching of the skin, which is sensitive to touch, and with stinging hot pains. There is usually feverishness and thirst and the pains are worsened by heat and relieved by cold. The remedy is used for insect stings, nettle rash, allergic conditions, blisters, whitlow (an abscess on the fingertip) and infections of the urinary tract, including cystitis, with stabbing hot pains. Also for urinary incontinence in elderly persons, fluid retention causing swelling of the eyelids or other areas, allergic conditions that cause sore throat and swallowing difficulty, and tonsillitis. The person often experiences hot, stabbing headaches and has dry skin. Apis is additionally valued as a remedy for swollen, painful inflammation of the joints as in arthritic conditions and for peritonitis and pleurisy. The symptoms are made worse by heat and touch, stuffy airless rooms following sleep and in the early evening. They improve in the fresh, cool open air, after taking a cold bath, or any cold application. A person suitable for the Apis remedy tends to expect high standards and may be rather irritable and hard to please. He (or she) likes to organise others and is jealous of his own domain, tending to be resentful of anyone new. Apis types may seem to be rushing around and working hard but may achieve very little as a result.

Argenticum nitricum

Argent. nit; silver nitrate, devil's stone, lunar caustic, hellstone

Silver nitrate is obtained from the mineral acanthite, which is a natural ore of silver. White silver nitrate crystals are derived from a chemical solution of the mineral ore and these are used to make the homeopathic remedy. Silver nitrate is poisonous in large doses and has antiseptic and caustic properties. In the past it was used to clean out wounds and prevent infection. In homeopathy, it is used to treat states of great anxiety, panic, fear or apprehension about a forthcoming event, e.g. taking an examination, having to perform a public role (speech-making, chairing a public meeting, acting, singing), going for an interview, or any activity involving scrutiny and criticism by others. It was also used as a remedy for digestive complaints including indigestion, abdominal pain, wind, nausea and headache. Often, there is a longing for sweet 'comfort' or other types of food. Argent. nit. may be given for laryngitis, sore throat and hoarseness, eye inflammation such as conjunctivitis, and period pains. Other types of pain, asthma and warts may benefit from Argent. nit.

Often, a person experiences symptoms mainly on the left side, and these are worse with heat and at night. Also, they are made worse by anxiety and overwork, emotional tension and resting on the left side. Pains are made worse with talking and movement. Symptoms improve in cold or cool fresh air and are relieved by belching. Pains are helped by applying pressure to the painful part. People suitable for Argent nit. are quick-witted and rapid in thought and action. They may appear outgoing and happy but are prey to worry, anxiety and ungrounded fears that make them tense. All the emotions are quick to surface, and Argent nit. people are able to put on an impressive performance. They enjoy a wide variety of foods, particularly salty and sweet things although these may upset the digestion. They have a fear of heights, crowds, of being burgled and of failure and arriving late for an appointment. Also, of serious illness, dying and madness. Argent. nit. people are generally slim and full of restless energy and tension. They may have deeply etched features and lines on the skin that make them appear older than their real age.

Arnica montana

Arnica; leopard's bane, sneezewort, mountain tobacco

Arnica is a native plant of woodland and mountainous regions of central Europe and Siberia. It has a dark brown root system from which a central stem arises, producing pairs of elongated green leaves and bright yellow flowers. If the flowers are crushed or bruised and a person then inhales the scent, this causes sneezing. All the fresh parts of the flowering plant are used to prepare the homeopathic remedy. It is a commonly used first aid remedy for symptoms relating to injury or trauma of any kind, e.g. bruising, swelling, pain and bleeding. It is also used to treat physical and mental shock. It is helpful following surgery, childbirth or tooth extraction, promoting healing, and also for gout, rheumatic joints with pain, heat and inflammation, sore sprained or strained muscles, concussion, and osteoarthritis. Taken internally, it is a remedy for black eyes, eye strain, skin conditions such as eczema and boils. Arnica is helpful in the treatment of whooping cough in children and also wetting the bed when the cause is nightmares. Symptoms are made worse with heat, touch and continued movement, and also with heat and resting for a long period. The symptoms improve when the person first begins to move and with lying down with the head at a lower level than the feet. A person suitable for this remedy tends to be solemn, fatalistic and subject to morbid fears. Arnica types usually deny the existence of any illness, even when obviously not well, and do not seek medical help, preferring to manage on their own.

Arsenicum album

Arsen. alb.; white arsenic trioxide

This is a widely used homeopathic remedy, the source being white arsenic trioxide derived from arsenopyrite, a metallic mineral ore of arsenic. Arsenic has been known for centuries as a poison and was once used as a treatment for syphilis. White arsenic trioxide used to be given to improve muscles and skin in animals such as horses. It is used to treat acute conditions of the digestive system and chest and mental symptoms of anxiety and fear. Hence it is a remedy for diarrhoea and vomiting caused by eating the wrong kinds of food; or food poisoning or overindulgence in alcohol. Also, for dehydration in children following gastroenteritis or feverish illness. It is a remedy for asthma and breathing difficulty, mouth ulcers, carbuncles (collections of boils), dry, cracked lips, burning skin, inflamed, watering stinging eyes and psoriasis. Also, for sciatica, shingles, sore throat and painful swallowing, candidiasis (fungal infection) of the mouth and motion sickness.

There may be oedema (retention of fluid) showing as a puffiness around the ankles.

An ill person who benefits from Arsen. alb. experiences burning pains but also feels cold. The skin may be either hot or cold to the touch. The symptoms are worse with cold in any form, including cold food and drink, and between midnight and 3 a.m. They are worse on the right side and if the person is near the coast. Symptoms improve with warmth, including warm drinks, gentle movement and lying down with the head raised. People suitable for Arsen. alb. are precise, meticulous and ambitious and loathe any form of disorder. They are always immaculately dressed and everything in their life is neat and tidy. However, they tend to have great worries, especially about their financial security and their own health and that of their family. They fear illness and dying, loss of financial and personal status, being burgled, darkness and the supernatural. Arsen. alb. people have strongly held views and do not readily tolerate contrary opinions or those with a more relaxed or disordered lifestyle. They enjoy a variety of different foods, coffee and alcoholic drinks. They are usually thin, with delicate, fine features and pale skin that may show worry lines. Their movements tend to be rapid and their manner serious and somewhat restless, although always polite.

Atropa belladonna

Belladonna, deadly nightshade, black cherry, devil's cherries, naughty man's cherries, devil's herb

Belladonna is a native plant of most of Europe although it is uncommon in Scotland. The plant is extremely poisonous, and many children have died as a result of being tempted to eat the shiny black berries of deadly nightshade. It is a stout, stocky plant with light brown roots, growing to about four feet high, with green oval leaves and pale purple, bell-shaped flowers. In medieval times, the plant had its place in the potions of witchcraft. Italian women used extracts of the plant as eye drops to widen the pupils of the eye and make them more beautiful (hence *bella donna*, which means 'beautiful woman'). The plant contains atropine, an alkaloid substance that induces paralysis of nerves and is used in orthodox medicine to relieve painful spasms and in ophthalmic (eye) procedures.

In homeopathy, the remedy is obtained from the pulped leaves and flowers. It was investigated and proved by Hahnemann as a treatment for scarlet fever. Belladonna is used to treat acute conditions that arise suddenly in which there is a throbbing, pulsing headache and red, flushed skin, high fever and staring wide eyes. The skin around the mouth and lips may be pale, but the tongue is a fiery red and the hands and feet are cold. It is used as a remedy for infectious diseases such as influenza, scarlet fever, measles, whooping cough, chicken pox, mumps and the early stages of pneumonia. It is also used for boils, earache (particularly on the right side and worse when the head is cold or wet), cystitis, boils, conjunctivitis, tonsillitis, inflammation of the kidneys, neuralgia (sharp pain along the course of a nerve) and sore throat. Other conditions that benefit from this remedy include labour pains, soreness of the breasts in breast-feeding, fever and teething in children, broken sleep and whitlow (an infection of a fingernail). The symptoms are worse at night and with lying down, and occur more intensely on the right side. Also, they are exacerbated by loud noises, bright lights, jarring of the body, touch or pressure and with cool surroundings.

They improve with sitting upright or standing and holding warm applications against the painful area. People suitable for belladonna usually enjoy good health, being fit, energetic and ready to tackle any task. They are amusing, sociable and popular when in good health. However, if they become ill the reverse is often true and they may be restless, irritable and possibly even violent.

Aurum metallicum

Aurum met.; gold

Gold was highly prized by Arabian physicians in the early Middle Ages who used it to treat heart disorders. In the early part of this century, it was used in the treatment of tuberculosis. Gold is now used in conventional medicine for some cancer treatments and for rheumatic and arthritic complaints. In homeopathy, pure gold is ground down to produce a fine powder, and it is used to treat both physical and mental symptoms. It is used as a remedy for congestive circulatory disorders and heart diseases including angina pectoris. The symptoms include a throbbing, pulsing headache, chest pain, breathlessness and palpitations. It is also used to treat liver disorders with symptoms of jaundice, painful conditions of bones and joints (especially the hip and knee), inflammation of the testes and an undescended testicle in small boys (especially if the right side is affected). It is a remedy for sinusitis and severe mental symptoms of despair, depression and thoughts of suicide. The person who is suitable for this remedy tends to drive himself very hard to the point of being a workaholic. He (or she) is excessively conscientious but usually feels that he has not done enough and is oversensitive to the criticism of other people. The person may come to regard himself as a failure and become severely clinically depressed or even suicidal. Symptoms are made worse by mental effort and concentration, or physical exercise, especially in the evening or night and by emotional upheaval. They improve with cold bathing, walking in the fresh air and with rest and quiet.

Bryonia alba

Bryonia, European white bryony, black-berried white bryony, wild hops

Bryony is a native plant of many parts of Europe and grows in England, although it is rarely found in Scotland. It has large, white, branched roots with swollen, expanded portions that are highly poisonous. The smell given off is unpleasant and, if eaten, the taste is very bitter and death soon follows. The tall stems of the plant climb up supports by means of corkscrew tendrils and round black berries are produced in the autumn.

Bryony was used by the physicians of ancient Greece and Rome and was described by Hippocrates. The homeopathic remedy is made from the fresh pulped root of the plant, and is mainly used for conditions producing acute stitch-like pains, which are made worse by even slight movement and relieved by rest. These ailments usually develop slowly and accompanying symptoms include dry skin, mouth and eyes with great thirst. It is used as a remedy for inflammation of the lining of joints in arthritic and rheumatic disorders with swelling, heat and pains. Also, for chest inflammation, pleurisy, chesty bronchitis and pneumonia with severe pain and dry, hacking cough. Digestive problems that are eased by Bryonia include indigestion, colic, constipation, nausea, vomiting and diarrhoea. Breast inflammation because of breast-feeding, colic in babies, gout and lumbago may be helped by Bryonia. The symptoms are made worse by movement and bending and improve with rest and pressure applied to the painful area. People suitable for Bryonia are hard-working, conscientious and reliable but have a dread of poverty. They tend to measure success in life in financial or materialistic terms. They cope badly with any threat to their security or lifestyle, becoming extremely worried, fretful and depressed.

Calcarea carbonica

Calc. carb.; calcium carbonate

This important homeopathic remedy is made from powdered mother-of-pearl, the beautiful, translucent inner layer of oyster shells. Calcium is an essential mineral in the body, being especially important for the healthy development of bones and teeth. The Calc. carb. remedy is used to treat a number of different disorders, especially those relating to bones and teeth, and also certain skin conditions and symptoms relating to the female reproductive system. It is a remedy for weak or slow growth of bones and teeth and fractures that take a long time to heal. Also, for teething problems in children, pains in bones, teeth and joints, headaches and eye inflammations affecting the right side, and ear infections with an unpleasant-smelling discharge. Premenstrual syndrome, heavy periods and menopausal disorders are helped by Calc. carb., and also chapped skin and eczema.

Calc. carb. may be used as a remedy for verruca (a type of wart) and thrush infections. People who benefit from Calc. carb. are very sensitive to the cold, particularly in the hands and feet and tend to sweat profusely. They suffer from fatigue and anxiety, and body secretions (sweat and urine) smell unpleasant. Children who benefit from Calc. carb. have recurrent ear, nose and throat infections, especially tonsillitis and glue ear. Symptoms are made worse by draughts and cold, damp weather and also at night. They are worse when the person first wakens up in the morning and for physical exercise and sweating. In women, symptoms are worse premenstrually. They improve in warm, dry weather and are better later on in the morning and after the person has eaten breakfast. People suitable for Calc. carb. are often overweight or even obese with a pale complexion. They are shy and very sensitive, quiet in company and always worried about what other people think of them. Calc. carb. people are hard-working, conscientious and reliable and easily upset by the suffering of others. They need constant reassurance from friends and family and tend to feel that they are a failure. Usually, Calc. carb. people enjoy good health but have a tendency for skeletal weakness. They enjoy a wide variety of different foods and tend to overeat, but are upset by coffee and milk. They are afraid of dying and serious illness, the supernatural, madness, being a failure and becoming poor, and they tend to be claustrophobic.

Calcarea fluorica

Calc. fluor.; fluorite, calcium fluoride, fluoride of lime

This homeopathic remedy is one of the Schussler tissue salts (*see* GLOSSARY). Calcium fluoride occurs naturally in the body in the enamel of the teeth, bones, skin and connective tissue. It is used to treat disorders of these body tissues or to maintain their elasticity. It is used to treat chronic lumbago, scars, and to prevent the formation of adhesions after operations, gout and arthritic nodules. Also, for rickets, slow growth of bones in children, enlarged adenoids that become stony because of persistent, recurrent respiratory tract infections and cataracts. It is used to strengthen weak tooth enamel and strained and stretched ligaments and muscles, e.g. around a joint. People suitable for Calc. fluor. are intelligent and punctual but tend to make mistakes through lack of planning. They benefit from the guidance of others to work efficiently and fear poverty and illness. They are often prone to piles, varicose veins, swollen glands and muscle and ligament strain. The manner of walking may be rapid with jerking of the limbs. Symptoms are made worse on beginning movement and in cold, damp, draughty conditions. They improve with warmth and heat and for continual gentle movement.

Calcarea phosphorica

Calc. phos., phosphate of lime, calcium phosphate

This homeopathic remedy is a SCHUSSLER TISSUE SALT (*see* Glossary) and calcium phosphate is the mineral that gives hardness to bones and teeth. It is obtained by a chemical reaction between dilute phosphoric acid and calcium hydroxide, when a white precipitate of calcium phosphate is formed. Since calcium phosphate is an essential mineral in the normal, healthy development of bones and teeth, it is used to treat disorders in these tissues. It is particularly helpful as a remedy for painful bones, difficult fractures that are slow to heal, teeth prone to decay, problems of bone growth and teething in children and 'growing pains'. Also, it is beneficial during convalescence when a person is weakened and tired after an illness, and for digestive problems including diarrhoea, stomach pains and indigestion. It may be used as a remedy for tonsillitis, sore throats and swollen glands. Children who benefit from this remedy tend to be thin, pale, miserable and fail to thrive, and are prone to sickness and headaches. They are often fretful and demanding. Adults are also unhappy and discontented with their circumstances, although endeavour to be friendly towards others. They are restless and need plenty of different activities and stimulation, hating routine and needing a good reason to get out of bed in the morning. Symptoms are made worse by any change in the weather, and in cold, wet conditions, e.g. thawing snow. Also for worry or grief and too much physical activity. Symptoms improve when the weather is warm and dry, in summer, and from taking a hot bath.

Calendula officinalis

Calendula, marigold, garden marigold, marygold

This is a familiar garden plant that grows well in all parts of the United Kingdom, having light green leaves and bright orange flowers. The plant has been known for centuries for its healing properties and was used in the treatment of various ailments. The parts used in homeopathy are the leaves and flowers, and the remedy is of value in first aid for its antiseptic and anti-inflammatory activity. It is used in the treatment of boils, stings, cuts and wounds, and to stem bleeding, often in the form of an ointment that can be applied to broken skin. It is helpful when applied to skin tears following childbirth. It is used in the form of an antiseptic tincture as a mouth wash and gargle after tooth extraction, for mouth ulcers or a septic sore throat. When taken internally it prevents suppuration (pus formation) and may be used for persistent chronic ulcers and varicose ulcers, fever and jaundice. It is a useful remedy in the treatment of children's ailments. The symptoms are made worse in damp, draughty conditions and cloudy weather and after eating. They improve with walking about and lying absolutely still.

Cantharis vesicatoria

Cantharis, Spanish fly

This remedy is derived from the body and wings of a bright green iridescent beetle that is found mainly in the southern parts of Spain and France. The beetle, *Cantharis vesicatoria*, secretes a substance called canthardin, which has irritant properties, is also poisonous and is an ancient remedy to cure warts. It was also used as an aphrodisiac, reputedly by the notorious Maquis de Sade. The beetles are dried and ground to produce a powder that is then used in homeopathy. It is an irritant, blistering agent acting externally on the part of the body to which it is applied and internally on the bladder, urinary tract and genital organs. Hence it is used to treat conditions in which there are stinging and burning pains. An accompanying symptom is often a great thirst but a reluctance to drink. It is used to treat cystitis with cutting hot pains on passing urine, urinary frequency with pain and other urinary infections. Also, certain inflammations of the digestive system in which there is abdominal distension and burning pains and diarrhoea. In general it is used as a remedy for conditions that worsen rapidly. It is a remedy for burns and scalds of the skin, including sunburn, insect stings, and rashes with spots that contain pus. Some mental symptoms are eased by Cantharis, including angry and irritable or violent behaviour, extreme anxiety and excessive sexual appetite. Symptoms are made worse with movement, touch and after drinking coffee or chilled water. They improve when gastrointestinal wind is eliminated and with warmth, at night time and with very light massage.

Carbo vegetabilis

Carbo veg., vegetable charcoal

The homeopathic remedy Carbo veg. is made from charcoal, which itself is obtained from heating or partially burning wood without oxygen. The charcoal is hard and black or dark grey, and is a form of carbon that is present in all living things. Charcoal has been made for centuries, and usually silver birch, beech or poplar trees are the source of wood that is used. The homeopathic remedy is used to treat a person who is run down, weak or exhausted, especially after a debilitating illness or operation. It is also used for postoperative shock, when there is a clammy, cold, pale skin but the person feels a sensation of heat or burning inside. It is helpful as a remedy for ailments of poor circulation such as varicose veins. Again, the skin tends to be pale, clammy and chilly with a bluish colour and the extremities feel cold. The legs may be puffy, and additional symptoms include hoarseness and laryngitis and lack of energy. Carbo veg. is a useful remedy for digestive problems, and carbon is also used for this purpose in orthodox medicine. Symptoms are those of indigestion, heartburn and flatulence with a sour taste in the mouth. Morning headaches with accompanying symptoms of nausea and giddiness or fainting may be relieved by Carbo veg., particularly if the cause is a large, heavy meal the night before. People suitable for this remedy often complain of a lack of energy and may indeed be physically and mentally exhausted, with poor powers of concentration and lapses of memory. They usually have fixed attitudes, with a lack of interest in news of the wider world. They do not like the night and are fearful of the supernatural. Symptoms are made worse by warm, moist weather, in the evening and night, and with lying down. They are also exacerbated after eating meals of fatty foods, coffee and milk and drinks of wine. They improve with burping and with circulating cool, fresh air.

Chamomilla

Camomile, common camomile, double camomile

A creeping and trailing plant that produces daisy-like flowers in summer and prefers dry, sandy soils. Camomiles are native to Britain and others part of northern Europe and have been used in medicine since ancient times, being described by Hippocrates. When walked on, it gives off an aromatic perfume and was gathered and strewn on the floor in medieval dwellings to counter unpleasant odours. It is prized for its many medicinal uses, the flowers and leaves both being used for a number of different ailments. Herbalists use camomile to treat skin conditions such as eczema, and for asthma and disturbed sleep. In homeopathy, it is used for its soothing and sedative effect on all conditions producing restlessness, irritability and pains. It is a useful remedy for children's complaints such as teething where the child is fretful and cries if put down, colicky pains and disturbed sleep. Also, for toothache, when one cheek is red and the other white, that is exacerbated by heat and relieved by cold. It is used to treat a blocked ear and earache, painful, heavy periods, and soreness and inflammation associated with breast-feeding. People suitable for this remedy are very sensitive to pain, which causes sweating or fainting, especially in children and women. They are irritable and fretful when ill. Symptoms are made worse if the person becomes angry or in cold winds and the open air. They improve if the person fasts for a time and if the weather is wet and warm. People who are suitable for camomile are noisy sleepers, in that they frequently cry out or talk while dreaming. If woken suddenly from sleep they are extremely irritable and they like to poke their feet out from the bed covers to keep them cool.

Chincona officinalis

Cinchona succirubra; china, Peruvian bark, Jesuit's bark

This homeopathic remedy, known as china, is obtained from the dried bark of the cinchona tree and contains quinine. The attractive evergreen cinchona, with its red bark, is a native of the hot tropical forests of South America, but it is also cultivated in India, Sri Lanka and southeast Asia. A preparation of powdered bark was used to treat a feverish illness suffered by the Countess of Cinchon, wife of the viceroy of Peru in 1638. After her recovery she publicised the remedy, and the tree was called cinchona from this time. The value of the bark as a cure for malaria had long been known and used by Jesuit priests. This was the first homeopathic substance tested and proved by Hahnemann on himself.

In modern homeopathy it is used mainly as a remedy for nervous and physical exhaustion resulting from chronic debilitating illnesses. It is used for weakness because of dehydration, sweating, chills and fever, and headaches that are relieved if firm pressure is applied. The person wants drinks during periods of chills and shivering rather than when feverish and hot. He or she usually has a washed-out unhealthy complexion with very sensitive skin. China is also used as a remedy for neuralgia, muscles that twitch because of extreme fatigue, bleeding, including nosebleeds, and tinnitus (noises in the ears). It has a helpful effect on the digestion and is used to treat gastro-intestinal wind, gall bladder disorders and digestive upset. Some mental symptoms are helped by this remedy, including irritability and tetchy behaviour that is out of character, apathy and loss of concentration and sleeplessness.

People who are suitable for this remedy tend to be artistic, imaginative and highly strung. They find it easier to empathise with the natural world rather than with the people around them. They are intense and dislike trivial conversation and fatty foods such as butter, but have a liking for alcoholic drinks. Their nature makes them prone to irritability and depression, and they tend to draw up grand schemes at night that are later abandoned. Symptoms are made better by warmth and plenty of sleep and by the application of steady continuous pressure to a painful area. They are made worse by cold, draughty weather, particularly in the autumn, and in the evening and night.

Citrullus colocynthis

Colocynth; bitter cucumber, bitter apple

The plant *Citrullus colocynthis* is a native of Turkey and is also found in parts of Asia and Africa, flourishing in dry, arid conditions. It produces yellow flowers and then yellow-orange smooth fruits, about the size of a large apple, which contain many seeds embedded in a whitish pulp. The homeopathic remedy colocynth is obtained from the dried fruits from which the seeds have been removed. This is then ground down to produce a powder. The fruit itself is poisonous, having a violent irritant effect on the digestive tract, causing severe, cramp-like pains, inflammation and bleeding. This is caused by the presence of a substance called colocynthin. According to tradition, Elisha, the Old Testament prophet, is said to have performed a miraculous transformation of the fruit during the famine in Gilgal, making it fit for the people to eat. In homeopathy, colocynth is used to treat colicky abdominal pains that may be accompanied by sickness and diarrhoea (including colic in young babies). Also, for neuralgia, especially of the face, sciatica, ovarian or kidney pain because of nerves, rheumatic disorders and headache.

People who are helped by colocynth are often reserved, with a tendency to bottle up anger. They have strong opinions about what is right and wrong, and may become quite agitated if someone else has a contrary viewpoint. Physical symptoms of colicky pains or neuralgia and upset stomach may follow on from becoming upset or angry. The symptoms are made worse when the person becomes irritated or angry and in cold, damp weather conditions. Also, eating meals and drinking exacerbate the symptoms. They are relieved by warmth and pressure on the painful part and drinking coffee. Abdominal flatulence also relieves the symptoms.

Cuprum metallicum

Cuprum met.; copper

Copper ore, which is found in rocks in many parts of the world, has been mined and used for many centuries in the manufacture of weapons, utensils and jewellery, etc. In earlier times, physicians made an ointment from the ground metal and this was applied to raw wounds to aid healing.

Cuprum metallicum

Copper is poisonous in large doses affecting the nervous system and causing convulsions, paralysis and possibly death because of its effects upon respiratory muscles. Toxic effects were recognised in those who worked with the metal and who developed wasting because of poor absorption of food, coughs and respiratory symptoms, and colicky pains. The ruddy, gold-coloured metal is ground to produce a fine red powder that is used in homeopathy to treat cramping, colicky pains in the abdomen, and muscular spasms in the calves of the legs, and in the feet and ankles. It is also used as a remedy for epilepsy and problems of breathing and respiration such as asthma, croup and whooping cough in which there are spasms. The person may turn blue because of the effort of breathing.

The symptoms are made worse by touch, hot, sunny weather and for keeping emotions bottled up. They improve with sweating and drinking cold fluids. People who benefit from Cuprum met. have mood swings that alternate from stubbornness to passivity, weepiness and depression. They tend to be serious people who judge themselves severely and keep their emotions very much suppressed. As babies or toddlers, they may be breath-holders who turn blue with anger or as a result of a tantrum. As children, some are destructive and others are loners who dislike the company of others.

Daphne mezereum

Daphne, spurge laurel, wild pepper, spurge olive, flowering spurge, dwarf bay

This poisonous plant is native to upland areas of Europe and is cultivated in the United Kingdom. It produces cheerful bright-red flowers and dark green leaves, and the bark is the part used in homeopathy. It is used to treat skin conditions characterised by blistering, especially erysipelas, shingles and varicose ulcers. Also, for any condition in which there is a persistent, dry cough and tightness around the chest and a mucus discharge from the nose. There may be burning pains that are worse at night.

Drosera rotundifolia

Drosera, sundew, youthwort, red rot, moor grass

This small, carnivorous (insect-eating) plant is found widely throughout Europe and in Britain, where it grows in the poor, acidic soils of bogs, damp uplands, moorlands and woodlands. It is a small plant growing close to the ground, and needs to trap insects for extra nutrients as the soil in which it grows is so poor. It is remarkable for its leaves, which are covered with long red hairs, each with a small, fluid-containing gland at the top. When the sun shines on the leaves it resembles dew, hence the name sundew. An insect landing on the leaf is trapped because this curls over and inwards, and the sticky fluid secreted by the hairs holds it fast. The secretion contains enzymes that digest the body and the nutrients are absorbed by the plant. The small, white flowers of sundew are fully open in the early morning but close up when the sun is shining strongly. In medieval times, the plant was used to treat tuberculosis and the plague, and it was employed as a remedy for skin disorders in early Asian medicine. It was noticed that sheep who inadvertently cropped sundew developed a paroxysmal type of cough like whooping cough. It was investigated and proved as a remedy for this illness in homeopathy, and the whole plant is used to prepare the medicine. Any condition in which there is a violent, dry, persistent barking cough of a spasmodic nature, as in whooping cough, benefits from the use of sundew, which has a particular action on the upper respiratory tract. Accompanying symptoms are gagging, sickness, sweating and nosebleeds. It is also used to treat bronchitis, asthma, corns and warts, growing pains and pains in the bones.

People who benefit from this remedy are restless and fearful of being alone when they are ill, and they tend to be stubborn and lack concentration. They are suspicious and may feel that others are talking about them or concealing bad news. They are sensitive to the supernatural and are afraid of ghosts. The symptoms are worse for being too warm in bed, after midnight, with crying, lying down, laughing, singing and talking. Also, for meals of cold food and drinks. Symptoms improve out in the fresh air, with walking or gentle exercise, sitting propped up in bed, with pressure applied to the painful part and in quiet surroundings.

Euphrasia officinalis

Euphrasia, eyebright

Eyebright is an attractive wild flower that is variable in size and grows widely throughout Europe, including Britain, and in North America. It has been known since medieval times as a remedy for inflammation of the eyes, and this remains its main use in homeopathy. The plant flourishes on well-drained, chalky soils and may be between two and eight inches in height, depending upon conditions. It is partly parasitic, deriving some nourishment from the roots of grass, and produces pretty white, purple-veined flowers with yellow centres. The whole plant and flowers are used in homeopathy, and the remedy is used to treat eye disorders characterised by redness, inflammation, watering, burning, stinging or itching. These include conjunctivitis, blepharitis (inflammation of eyelids), injuries to the eye and dry eyes. It is also used as a remedy for allergic conditions such as hay fever, in which the eyes are very much affected, and colds producing eye symptoms. It is a remedy for the early stages of measles, headaches, some menstrual problems and inflammation of the prostate gland in men. Symptoms are worse in the evening, in windy and warm weather and for being inside. They improve in subdued light, with drinking a cup of coffee and with cold applications.

Ferrum phosphoricum

Ferrum phos.; ferric phosphate of iron, iron phosphate

Ferrum phos. is one of the SCHUSSLER TISSUE SALTS (*see* GLOSSARY), and the iron phosphate powder is obtained by chemical reaction between sodium phosphate, sodium acetate and iron sulphate. Iron is a very important substance in the body, being found in the haemoglobin pigment of red blood cells that transports oxygen to all the tissues and organs. The homeopathic remedy is used to treat the early stages of infections, inflammations and feverish conditions, before any other particular symptoms occur. It is used to treat colds and coughs in which there may be a slowly developing fever, headache, nosebleeds, bronchitis, hoarseness and loss of the voice, earache and rheumatic pains. Digestive symptoms such as sour indigestion, inflammation of the stomach (gastritis), and vomiting and some disorders of menstruation are helped by this remedy. It is also used to treat the early symptoms of dysentery. The person tends to be pale but is prone to flushing, and feels cold in the early afternoon. There may be a rapid weak pulse. Symptoms are worse at night and in the early morning between 4 a.m. and 6 a.m. Also, they are worse for heat and hot sun, movement and jarring of the body, pressure and touch and resting on the right side and suppressing sweating by the use of deodorants, etc. Symptoms improve for cold applications and with gentle movements. People who are suitable for Ferrum phos. tend to be thin and pale but may be liable to flush easily. They are intelligent and quick to absorb new concepts, having plenty of original ideas of their own. They may be prone to digestive and respiratory complaints, stomach upsets and coughs and colds.

Gelsemium sempervirens

Gelsemium, yellow jasmine, false jasmine, Carolina jasmine, wild woodbine

This attractive climbing plant is a native of the southern United States and parts of Mexico. It has a woody stem that twists around any available tree trunk, and grows on stream banks and on the sea coast. It produces attractive, large, bell-shaped, perfumed yellow flowers in the early spring, which belie the poisonous nature of the plant. It has an underground stem, or rhizome, from which arise a tangle of yellow roots that have an aromatic smell. The root is the part used in homeopathy and, if eaten in significant amounts, it affects the central nervous system, causing paralysis and possible death through failure of the nerves and muscles of the respiratory system. In homeopathy it is used to treat both physical and mental symptoms. The physical ailments treated mainly involve the nervous and respiratory systems. These include headaches that are worsened with bright light and movement, multiple sclerosis, eye pain, especially on the right side, sore throat and influenza-like symptoms, earache and feverish muscular pains. Accompanying symptoms include chills and shivering, flushed face and malaise. It is used to treat some menstrual problems including pain. Mental symptoms that are helped by Gelsemium include fears and phobias with symptoms of fatigue, weakness, trembling and apprehension. These fears may arise before an examination, interview or public performance (stage fright). Excitement or fear that causes the heart to skip a beat and extreme anxiety causing sleeplessness are helped by Gelsemium. Symptoms are made worse in the sun and in warm, moist, humid weather or damp and fog. They are also worse with smoking and for excitement, anticipation, stress or bad news. Symptoms improve with movement in the fresh air and after sweating and drinking alcohol or a stimulant drink. They improve after urinating—a large quantity of pale urine is usually passed. People suitable for Gelsemium tend to be well-built with a blue-tinged skin and often complain of feeling weak and tired. They are beset by fears, and may be cowardly and too fearful to lead or enjoy a normal active life.

Graphites

Graphite; black pencil lead

Graphite is a form of carbon that is the basis of all life. It is found in older igneous or metamorphic rocks, such as granite and marble, and is mined for its industrial uses, e.g. in batteries, motors, pencil leads, cleaning and lubricating fluids. It was investigated and proved by Hahnemann after he learned that it was being used by some factory workers to heal cold sores. The powder used in homeopathy is ground graphite, and it is mainly used for skin disorders that may be caused by metabolic imbalances and stomach ulcers. It is a remedy for eczema, psoriasis, acne, rough, dry skin conditions with pustules or blisters, scarring and thickened cracked nails and cold sores. Also, for stomach ulcers caused by a thinning or weakness in the lining of the stomach wall, problems caused by excessive catarrh, loss of hair, and cramping pains or numbing of the feet and hands. In women it is used to treat some menstrual problems. The symptoms are worse in draughty, cold and damp conditions and for eating sweet meals or sea foods. Also, the use of steroids for skin complaints and, in women, during menstruation. Symptoms are often worse on the left side. They improve with warmth as long as the air is fresh and it is not stuffy, when it is dark and for eating and sleep. People suitable for Graphites are usually well-built and may be overweight, often having dark hair. They like to eat well but lack physical fitness, and sweat or flush with slight exertion. They are prone to dry, flaky skin conditions that may affect the scalp. Graphites people are usually lethargic and may be irritable, lacking in concentration for intellectual activities. They are prone to mood swings and subject to bouts of weeping, especially when listening to music. A Graphites person feels that he or she is unlucky and is inclined to self-pity, often feeling fearful and timid.

Guaiacum officinale

Guaiac, resin of lignum vitae

This attractive evergreen tree is a native of the West Indies and the northern coastal regions of South America. The tree grows to a height of 40-60 feet and produces striking, deep blue flowers. The part used in homeopathy is a resin obtained from the wood. The wood is unusual in being very dense, which means that it sinks in water, and this property caused much interest when it was first discovered in the Middle Ages. The resin is obtained by firing the cut log, and the melted resin then flows out of a hole made in the wood and is collected. This is allowed to cool and harden, and it is usually exported in large blocks that split readily into glassy fragments. The remedy is used to treat inflammation of the pharynx (pharyngitis) and tonsillitis, being very helpful in relieving painful soreness of the throat. It is particularly indicated where there is foul-smelling sputum and sweating. It is also a remedy for gout and rheumatic conditions with severe and stabbing joint pains. The symptoms are made worse by extremes of heat and cold and damp weather, and also with movement. They may be relieved by rest and keeping warm.

Hamamelis virginiana

Hamamelis, witch hazel, spotted alder, snapping hazelnut, winterbloom

This plant is a native of the eastern United States and Canada but it is also grown in Europe. It is a shrub with grey-green leaves and yellow flowers that appear in the autumn. The part used in homeopathy is the bark of stems and twigs and the outer part of the fresh root. This has the effect of causing body tissues, especially blood vessels, to contract, and it is used to arrest bleeding. Its curative properties were known to the native North American Indians, and it was first investigated and proved in homeopathy by Dr Hering. Its main effect is on the blood circulation of the veins, particularly when the walls of the vessels are inflamed and weakened, and bleeding does not stop easily. It is used as a remedy for haemorrhoids (piles) with bleeding, varicose veins and ulcers, phlebitis (inflamed veins), nosebleeds, heavy periods, internal bleeding and pain associated with bruising or bleeding. Some headaches are helped by Hamamelis and, also, mental symptoms of depression, irritability and impatience. The symptoms are made worse by warmth and moisture and with physical activity. They improve out in the fresh air and for concentrating on a particular task or event and for conversation, thinking and reading.

Hepar sulphuris calcareum

Hepar sulph.; sulphide of calcium

This remedy is impure calcium sulphide, which is obtained by heating crushed and powdered oyster shells with flowers of sulphur. This is an old remedy that was, at one time, applied externally to treat swellings caused by tuberculosis, gout, rheumatism and thyroid disorders (goitre) and also itching skin. It was investigated and proved by Hahnemann as a remedy for the toxic effects of mercury, which was widely used by contemporary physicians. It is now used to treat infections and any condition where there is a discharge of foul-smelling pus. It is used to treat skin conditions where the skin is highly sensitive to touch, such as boils and acne, and also, tonsillitis, sinusitis, earache, sore throat, hoarseness and laryngitis, mouth ulcers and cold sores. A wheezing, croup-like type of cough or chesty cough that may develop into a cold or influenza is helped by Hepar sulph. This remedy helps those who, when ill, tend to produce bodily secretions that have an unpleasant sour smell. During illness, those who benefit from this remedy are irritable, difficult to please and easily offended. They are difficult patients who make unreasonable demands and hate noise or disturbance, being touched or cold air. Symptoms are worse for cold and for getting chilled when undressing during winter and for touch. They improve with warmth and warm applications and for covering the head and for eating a meal. People suitable for Hepar sulph. tend to be overweight, lethargic, pale-skinned and often depressed. They feel that life has dealt with them harshly and feel the symptoms of illness and pain acutely. They may appear to be calm but tend to be anxious and restless.

Hypericum perforatum

Hypericum, St John's wort

A perennial herbaceous plant that is a native of Britain, Europe and Asia, but is cultivated throughout the world. It grows between one and three feet in height, producing elongated, oval dark green leaves that appear to be covered in minute spots or holes (hence *perforatum*, or perforate). In fact, these are minute oil-secreting glands that secrete a bright red solution. The large, bright yellow flowers appear in June, July and August and have small black dots around the edges of the petals. The crushed flowers produce a blood-coloured juice that was used, in early times, to treat raw wounds. It was also believed that the plant could be hung up to ward off evil spirits (the name

Hypericum perforatum

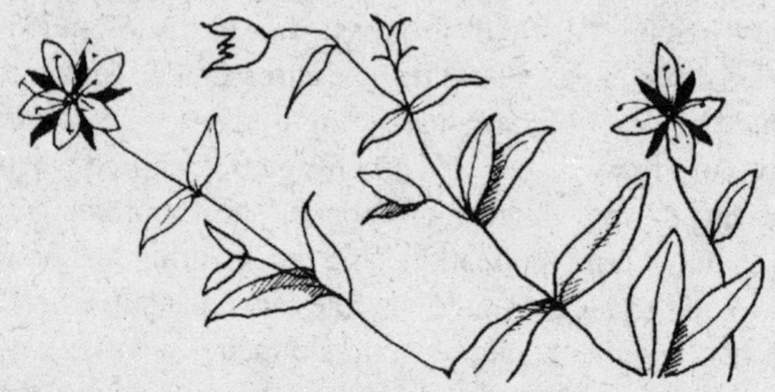

Hypericum being derived from the Greek, meaning 'over an apparition'). There are two traditions associated with the common name, St John's wort. One links the plant with 29 August, believed to be the anniversary of the execution of St John the Baptist. The other is that the plant is named after an ancient order of knights going back to the time of the Crusades, the knights of St John of Jerusalem.

The whole fresh green plant and flowers are used in homeopathy to produce the mother tincture. It is mainly used to treat damage to nerves and nerve pain following accidental injury. Typically, there are shooting, stabbing pains that radiate upwards, and it is indicated especially where there are many nerve endings concentrated in a particular part of the body, e.g. the fingers and toes. It is very effective in pains associated with the spinal nerves and spinal cord, concussion, head or eye injuries. It is also a remedy for wounds and lacerations producing stabbing pains indicating nerve damage, and accidental crushing injuries. It is useful for bites, stings, splinters and puncture wounds, toothache and pain following dental extractions. In addition, it is a treatment for asthma and some digestive complaints of indigestion, sickness and diarrhoea. It is sometimes helpful in the treatment of piles, or haemorrhoids, and some menstrual problems with accompanying headache. The symptoms are made worse by cold, damp or foggy weather, before a storm, by getting chilled when undressing, by touch and by a close, stuffy atmosphere. Symptoms improve when the person remains still and tilts the head backwards.

Ignatia amara

Agnate; *Strychnos ignatii*, St Ignatius' bean

Ignatia amara is a large tree that is native to the Philippine Islands, China and the East Indies. The tree has many branches and twining stems and produces stalked white flowers. Later, seed pods are produced, each containing ten to twenty large, oval seeds, that are about one inch long and are embedded in pulp. The seeds are highly poisonous and contain strychnine, which affects the central nervous system. Similar active constituents and properties are found in nux vomica. The tree is named after the founder of the Jesuits, Ignatius Loyola (1491-1556), and Spanish priests belonging to this order brought the seeds to Europe during the 1600s. The homeopathic remedy is made from the powdered seeds and is used especially for emotional symptoms. It is used for grief, bereavement, shock and loss, particularly when a person is having difficulty coming to terms with his or her feelings and is inclined to suppress the natural responses. Accompanying symptoms include sleeplessness, anger and hysteria. Similar emotional and psychological problems are helped by this remedy, including anxiety and fear, especially of appearing too forward to others, a tendency to burst into fits of crying, self-doubt, pity and blame, and depression. Nervous tension headaches and digestive upsets, feverish symptoms, chills and pains in the abdomen may be helped by Ignatia. Some problems associated with menstruation, especially sharp pains or absence of periods are relieved by this remedy, as are conditions with changeable symptoms. These are worse in cold weather or conditions, with emotional trauma, being touched, for smoking and drinking coffee. They improve with warmth, moving about, eating, lying on the side or area that is painful and after passing urine.

The person for whom Ignatia is suitable is usually female and with a tendency towards harsh, self criticism and blame; she is usually a creative artistic person, highly sensitive but with a tendency to suppress the emotions. She is perceptive and intelligent but inclined to be hysterical and subject to erratic swings of mood. Typically, the person expects a high standard in those she loves. The person enjoys dairy products, bread and sour foods but sweets, alcoholic drinks and fruit upset her system. She is afraid of crowds, tends to be claustrophobic, and fears being burgled. Also, she is afraid of being hurt emotionally, and is very sensitive to pain. The person is usually dark-haired and of slim build with a worried expression and prone to sighing, yawning and excessive blinking.

Ipecacuanha

Ipecac.; *Cephaelis ipecacuanha*, *Psychotria ipecacuanha*, the ipecac plant

This plant is a native of South America, particularly Brazil, Bolivia and New Grenada. The plant contains the alkaloids emetine and cephaeline, and different varieties contain differing proportions of these alkaloids. The root is the part used in homeopathy, and the preparations may be in a number of different forms. It is used to treat conditions where the main symptoms are nausea and vomiting, which are intractable and persistent, e.g. motion sickness and morning sickness. It is also used as a remedy for bronchitis, breathlessness because of the presence of fluid in the lung, whooping cough and heart failure. The symptoms are made worse by cold weather and lying down, and after a meal of pork or veal. They improve in the fresh open air and while resting with the eyes shut.

Kalium bichromicum

Kali bich.; potassium dichromate, potassium bichromate

This substance has several uses in industry (e.g. in the preparations of dyes and in batteries) as well as its medicinal purposes. The crystals of potassium dichromate are bright orange and are prepared from a chemical reaction involving the addition of a solution of potassium chromate to an acid. It is used for discharges of mucus and disorders of the mucous membranes, particularly involving the vagina and genital and urinary tracts, throat, nose and stomach. The remedy is useful for catarrhal colds and sinusitis, feelings of fullness and pressure, headache, migraine and glue ear. Also, for joint and rheumatic disorders with pains that may move about or even disappear. People who benefit from this remedy are highly sensitive to cold and chills when ill, but also experience a worsening of symptoms in hot, sunny conditions. They tend to be people who adhere very closely to a regular routine and may be somewhat rigid and inflexible. They like everything to be done properly down to the smallest detail and are law-abiding, moral and conformist. Symptoms are worse during the summer and also in wet and chilly conditions. They are at their height in the early hours of the morning between 3 and 5 a.m., and also on first waking up. Drinking alcohol and becoming chilled while taking off clothes exacerbates the symptoms. They improve with moving around and after eating a meal. Also, symptoms improve with warmth and heat (but not hot sun) and after vomiting.

Kalium iodatum

Kali iod.; *Kali hydriodicum*, potassium iodide

This is prepared by chemical reaction from potassium hydroxide and iodine and is an old remedy for syphilis. It is recommended that potassium iodide should be added to animal feed concentrates and table salt to prevent deficiency in iodine. The homeopathic remedy is used to relieve catarrh in those who are prone to chesty conditions. It is also used to treat swollen glands, sore throats, sinusitis, hay fever and influenza-type infections. It is used to treat male prostate gland disorders. The symptoms tend to improve with movement and from being out in the fresh air. They are made worse by heat and touch and are at their most severe between two and five in the early morning. People who suit this remedy tend to be dogmatic, knowing exactly what they think about a particular subject. They may be irritable or bad-tempered and not easy to get along with. They have a preference for cool rather than warm or hot weather.

Kalium phosphoricum

Kali phos.; potassium phosphate, phosphate of potash

This remedy is one of the SCHUSSLER TISSUE SALTS (*see* GLOS-

SARY), and it is obtained from a chemical reaction between dilute phosphoric acid and solution of potassium carbonate. Potassium carbonate is derived from potash, the white powder that is left when wood is burnt completely. Potassium is an essential element in the body, vital for the healthy functioning of nerve tissue. Kali phos. is used to treat mental and physical exhaustion and depression, particularly in young persons in whom it may have been caused by too much work or studying. Accompanying symptoms include jumping at noise or interruption and a desire to be alone. Also, there may be a pus-containing discharge from the bladder, vagina, bowels or lungs and extreme muscular fatigue. They may suffer from gnawing hunger pains, anxiety, insomnia, tremor and have a tendency to perspire on the face when excited or after a meal. People who are suitable for Kali phos. are usually extrovert, hold clearly formed ideas and are easily exhausted. They become distressed by bad news, including that which does not affect them directly, such as a disaster in another country. They tend to crave sweet foods and dislike bread. Symptoms are made worse by any anxiety, in cold, dry weather and in winter and on drinking cold drinks. Also, they are exacerbated by noise, conversation, touch and physical activity. Symptoms improve with heat, gentle exercise, in cloudy conditions and after eating.

Lachesis

Trigonocephalus lachesis, *Lachesis muta*, venom of the bushmaster or surukuku snake

This South African snake produces a deadly venom that may prove instantly fatal because of its effects upon the heart. The venom causes the blood to thin and flow more freely, hence increasing the likelihood of haemorrhage. Even a slight bite bleeds copiously with a risk of blood poisoning or septicaemia. The snake is a ferocious hunter, and its African name, surukuku, describes the sound it makes while in pursuit of prey. The properties of the venom were investigated by the eminent American homeopathic doctor Constantine Hering during the 1800s. He tested and proved the remedy on himself. It is effective in treating a variety of disorders, particularly those relating to the blood circulation and where there is a risk of blood poisoning, or septicaemia. It is used to treat varicose veins and problems of the circulation indicated by a bluish tinge to the skin. The remedy is useful for those suffering from a weak heart or angina, palpitations and an irregular, fast or weak pulse. There may be symptoms of chest pain and breathing difficulty. It is of great benefit in treating uterine problems, particularly premenstrual congestion and pain that is relieved once the period starts. It is also an excellent remedy for menopausal symptoms, especially hot flushes, and for infections of the bladder and rectum. It is used to treat conditions and infections where symptoms are mainly on the left side, such as headache or stroke. It is also used as a treatment for sore throats and throat infections, tonsillitis, lung abscess, boils, ulcers, wounds that heal slowly, vomiting because of appendicitis and digestive disorders, fevers with chills and shivering, nosebleeds and bleeding piles.

It is used to treat severe symptoms of measles and serious infections including scarlet fever and smallpox. Symptoms are made worse by touch and after sleep and by tight clothing. They are worse for hot drinks and baths, exposure to hot sun or direct heat in any form. For women, symptoms are worse during the menopause. They improve for being out in the fresh air and drinking cold drinks and for release of normal bodily discharges. People suitable for Lachesis tend to be intelligent, creative, intense and ambitious. They have strong views about politics and world affairs and may be impatient of the views of others. They may be somewhat self-centred, possessive and jealous, which can cause problems in close relationships with others. They dislike being tied down and so may be reluctant to commit themselves to a relationship. Lachesis people have a liking for sour pickled foods, bread, rice and oysters and alcoholic drinks. They like coffee, but hot drinks and wheat-based food tends to upset them. They have a fear of water, people they do not know, being burgled and of dying or being suffocated. Lachesis people may be somewhat overweight and are sometimes red-haired and freckled. Alternatively, they may be thin and dark-haired, pale and with a lot of energy. Children tend to be somewhat jealous of others and possessive of their friends, which can lead to naughty or trying behaviour.

Ledum palustre

Ledum; marsh tea, wild rosemary

Wild rosemary is an evergreen shrub that grows in the bogs and cold upland conditions of the northern United States, Canada and northern Europe, especially Scandinavia, Ireland and parts of Asia. The bush produces elongated, dark green leaves, about one or two inches long, that are smooth and shiny on the upper surface but underneath are covered with brown woolly hairs. ('Ledum' is derived from the Greek word *ledos*, meaning 'woolly robe'). The leaves contain a volatile, aromatic oil like camphor, and the plant has been used for centuries by Scandinavian people to repel insects, moths and mice. The plant produces attractive white flowers and is valued for its antiseptic properties. The fresh parts of the plant are gathered, dried and ground to make a powder used in homeopathy, and it is a valuable first aid remedy. It is taken internally for animal bites, insect stings, lacerations and wounds in which there is bruising and sharp stabbing pains. There is usually inflammation, redness, swelling and throbbing accompanied by feverish symptoms of chills and shivering. It is additionally used as a remedy for gout in the big toe, rheumatic pains in the feet that radiate upwards, hot, painful, stiff joints and tendons but with cold skin. People who benefit from this remedy tend to get hot and sweaty at night when ill, and usually throw off the bed coverings. They often have itchy skin on the feet and ankles and have a tendency to sprain their ankles. When ill, they are irritable and hard to please or may be withdrawn, and do not want the company of others. The symptoms are made worse by warmth or heat, touch and at night. They improve with cold applications to the painful part and for cool conditions.

Lycopodium clavatum

Lycopodium; club moss, wolf's claw, vegetable sulphur, stag's-horn moss, running pine

This plant is found throughout the northern hemisphere, in high moorlands, forests and mountains. The plant produces spore cases on the end of upright forked stalks, which contain the spores. These produce yellow dust or powder that is resistant to water and was once used as a coating on pills and tablets to keep them separate from one another. The powder was also used as a constituent of fireworks. It has been used medicinally for many centuries, as a remedy for digestive disorders and kidney stones in Arabian countries and in the treatment of gout. The powder and spores are collected by shaking the fresh, flowering stalks of the plant, and its main use in homeopathy is for digestive and kidney disorders. It is used to treat indigestion, heartburn, the effects of eating a large meal late at night, sickness, nausea, wind, bloatedness and constipation. Also, in men, for kidney stones, with the production of a red-coloured urine containing a sand-like sediment and enlarged prostate gland. It is used in the treatment of some problems of male impotence and bleeding haemorrhoids, or piles. Symptoms that occur on the right side are helped by Lycopodium, and the patient additionally tends to crave sweet, comfort foods, nettle rash, psoriasis affecting the hands, fatigue because of illness, ME (myalgic encephalomyelitis), some types of headache, cough and sore throat are relieved by this remedy. It is used to relieve emotional states of anxiety, fear and apprehension caused by chronic insecurity or relating to forthcoming events, such as taking an examination or appearing in public (stage fright). Also, night terrors, sleeplessness, shouting or talking in the sleep and being frightened on first waking up can all benefit from this treatment.

The symptoms are worse between 4 p.m. and 8 p.m. and in warm, stuffy rooms and with wearing clothes that are too tight. They are also worse in the early morning between 4 a.m. and 8 a.m., for eating too much and during the spring. They improve outside in cool fresh air, after a hot meal or drink and with loosening tight clothing, with light exercise and at night. People suitable for Lycopodium tend to be serious, hard-working and intelligent, often in professional positions. They seem to be self-possessed and confident but are in reality rather insecure with a low self-opinion. They are impatient of what they perceive as being weakness and are not tolerant or sympathetic of illness. Lycopodium people are sociable but may keep their distance and not get involved; they may be sexually promiscuous. They have a great liking for sweet foods of all kinds and enjoy hot meals and drinks. They are easily filled but may carry on eating regardless of this and usually complain of symptoms on the right side. Lycopodium people are afraid of being left on their own, of failure in life, of crowds, darkness and the supernatural, and tend to be claustrophobic. They are often tall, thin and pale with receding hair or hair that turns grey early in life. They may be bald, with a forehead lined with worry lines and a serious appearance. They tend to have weak muscles and are easily tired after physical exercise. They may have a tendency to unconsciously twitch the muscles of the face and to flare the nostrils.

Mercurius solubilis

Merc. sol.; quicksilver

The mineral cinnabar, which is found in volcanic crystalline rocks, is an important ore of mercury and is extracted for a variety of uses, including dental fillings and in thermometers. Mercury is toxic in large doses, and an affected person produces great quantities of saliva and suffers repeated bouts of vomiting. Mercury has been used since ancient times and was once given as a remedy for syphilis. A powder of precipitate of mercury is obtained from dissolving liquid mercury in a dilute solution of nitric acid, and this is the source of the remedy used in homeopathy. It is used as a remedy for conditions that produce copious bodily secretions that often smell unpleasant, with accompanying symptoms of heat or burning and a great sensitivity to temperature. It is used as a remedy for fevers with profuse, unpleasant sweating, bad breath, inflammation of the gums, mouth ulcers, candidiasis (fungal infection) of the mouth, infected painful teeth and gums, and excessive production of saliva. Also, for a sore infected throat, tonsillitis, mumps, discharging infected ear, and a congested severe headache and pains in the joints. It is good for eye complaints, including severe conjunctivitis, allergic conditions with a running nose, skin complaints that produce pus-filled pustules, spots, and ulcers, including varicose ulcers. The symptoms are made worse by extremes of heat and cold and also by wet and rapidly changing weather. They are worse at night and for sweating and being too hot in bed.

Symptoms improve with rest and in comfortable temperatures where the person is neither too hot nor too cold. People suitable for Merc. sol. tend to be very insecure although they have an outwardly calm appearance. They are cautious and reserved with other people and consider what they are about to say before speaking so that conversation may seem laboured. Merc. sol. types do not like criticism of any kind and may suddenly become angry if someone disagrees with their point of view. They tend to be introverted, but their innermost thoughts may be in turmoil. They tend to be hungry and enjoy bread and butter, milk and other cold drinks but dislike alcohol with the exception of beer. They usually do not eat meat and do not have a sweet tooth. They dislike coffee and salt. Merc. sol. people often have fair hair with fine, unlined skin and an air of detachment. They are afraid of dying and of mental illness leading to insanity, and worry about the wellbeing of their family. They fear being burgled and are afraid or fearful during a thunderstorm.

Natrum muriaticum

Natrum mur.; common salt, sodium chloride

Salt has long been prized for its seasoning and preservative qualities, and Roman soldiers were once paid in salt, such was its value (the word 'salary' comes from the Latin word *salarium*, which refers to this practice). Sodium and chlorine are essential chemicals in the body, being needed for many metabolic processes, particularly the functioning of nerve tissue. In fact, there is seldom a need to add salt to food as usually enough is present naturally in a healthy, well-balanced diet. (An exception is when people are working very hard physically in a hot climate and losing a lot of salt in sweat). However, people and many other mammals frequently have a great liking for salt. If the salt/water balance in the body is disturbed, a person soon becomes very ill and may even die.

In ancient times, salt was usually obtained by boiling sea water, but natural evaporation around the shallow edges of salt lakes results in deposits of rock salt being formed. Rock salt is the usual source of table salt and also of the remedy used in homeopathy. This remedy has an effect on the functioning of the kidneys and the salt/water balance of body fluids, and is used to treat both mental and physical symptoms. Emotional symptoms that benefit from Natrum mur. include sensitivity and irritability, tearfulness and depression, suppressed grief and premenstrual tension. Physical ailments that respond to this remedy are often those in which there is a thin, watery discharge of mucus and in which symptoms are made worse by heat. Hence Natrum mur. is used in the treatment of colds with a runny nose or other catarrhal problems. Also, for some menstrual and vaginal problems, headaches and migraines, cold sores, candidiasis (fungal infection) of the mouth, mouth ulcers, inflamed and infected gums and bad breath. Some skin disorders are helped by Natrum mur., including verruca (a wart on the foot), warts, spots and boils, and cracked, dry lips. It may be used in the treatment of fluid retention with puffiness around the face, eyelids and abdomen, etc, urine retention, constipation, anal fissure, indigestion, anaemia and thyroid disorders (goitre). When ill, people who benefit from this remedy feel cold and shivery, but their symptoms are made worse, or even brought on, by heat. Heat, whether from hot sun and fire or a warm, stuffy room, exacerbate the symptoms, which also are made worse by cold and thundery weather. They are worse on the coast from the sea breeze, and in the morning between 9 and 11 o'clock. Too much physical activity and the sympathy of others exacerbate the symptoms. They improve in the fresh, open air and for cold applications or a cold bath or swim. Also, sleeping on a hard bed and sweating and fasting make the symptoms better. People suitable for Natrum mur. are often women who are highly sensitive, serious-minded, intelligent and reliable. They have high ideals and feel things very deeply, being easily hurt and stung by slights and criticism. They need the company of other people but, being so sensitive, can actually shun them for fear of being hurt. They are afraid of mental illness leading to loss of self-control and insanity, and of dying. Also, they fear the dark, failure in work, crowds, being burgled and have a tendency to be claustrophobic. They worry about being late and are fearful during a thunderstorm. Merc. sol. people tend to become introverted and react badly to the criticism of others. They are highly sensitive to the influence of music, which easily moves them to tears. Natrum mur. people are usually of squat or solid build with dark or fairish hair. They are prone to reddened, watery eyes as though they have been crying, and a cracked lower lip. The face may appear puffy and shiny with an air of stoicism.

Nux vomica

Strychnos nux vomica, poison nut, Quaker buttons

The *Strychnos nux vomica* tree is a native of India but also grows in Burma, Thailand, China and Australia. It produces small, greenish-white flowers and, later, apple-sized fruits, containing small, flat, circular pale seeds covered in fine hair. The seeds, bark and leaves are highly poisonous, containing strychnine, and have been used in medicine for many centuries. In medieval times, the seeds were used as a treatment for the plague. Strychnine has severe effects upon the nervous system but in minute amounts can help increase urination and aid digestion. The seeds are cleaned and dried and used to produce the homeopathic remedy. Nux vomica is used in the treatment of a variety of digestive complaints, including cramping, colicky abdominal pains, indigestion, nausea and vomiting, diarrhoea and constipation. Also, indigestion or stomach upset caused by overindulgence in alcohol or rich food, and piles, which cause painful contractions of the rectum. Sometimes these complaints are brought on by a tendency to keep emotions, particularly anger, suppressed and not allowing it to show or be expressed outwardly. Nux vomica is a remedy for irritability, headache and migraine, colds, coughs and influenza-like symptoms of fever, aching bones and muscles and chills and shivering. It is a useful remedy for women who experience heavy, painful periods that may cause fainting, morning sickness during pregnancy and pain in labour. It is also used to treat urinary frequency and cystitis.

The type of person who benefits from this remedy is frequently under stress and experiences a periodic flare-up of symptoms. The person may be prone to indigestion and heartburn, gastritis and stomach ulcer, and piles, or haemorrhoids. The person usually has a tendency to keep everything bottled up but has a passionate nature and is liable to outbursts of anger. Nux vomica people are very ambitious and competitive, demanding a high standard of themselves and others and intolerant of anything less than perfection. They enjoy challenges and using their wits to keep one step ahead. Often they are to be found as managers, company directors, scientists, etc, at the cutting edge of their particular occupation. They are ungracious and irritable when ill and cannot abide the criticism of others. This type of person is afraid of being a failure at work and fears or dislikes crowded public places. He or she is afraid of dying. The person enjoys rich, fattening foods containing cholesterol and spicy meals, alcohol and coffee, although these upset the digestive system. Symptoms are worse in cold, windy, dry weather and in winter and in the early morning between 3 and 4 a.m. They are aggravated by certain noises, music, bright lights and touch, eating (especially spicy meals) and overwork of mental faculties. Nux vomica people usually look serious, tense and are thin with a worried expression. They have sallow skin and tend to have dark shadows beneath the eyes.

Phosphorus

Phos; white phosphorus

Phosphorus is an essential mineral in the body found in the genetic material (DNA), bones and teeth. White phosphorus is extremely flammable and poisonous and was once used in the manufacture of matches and fireworks. As it tends to catch fire spontaneously when exposed to air, it is stored under water. In the past it has been used to treat a number of disorders and infectious diseases such as measles. In homeopathy, the remedy is used to treat nervous tension caused by stress and worry, with symptoms of sleeplessness, exhaustion and digestive upset. Often there are pains of a burning nature in the chest or abdomen. It is a remedy for vomiting and nausea, heartburn, acid indigestion, stomach ulcer and gastroenteritis. It is also used to treat bleeding, e.g. from minor wounds, the gums, nosebleeds, gastric and profuse menstrual bleeding.

Severe coughs, which may be accompanied by retching, vomiting and production of a blood-tinged phlegm, are treated with Phos. as well as some other severe respiratory complaints. These include pneumonia, bronchitis, asthma and laryngitis. Styes that tend to recur and poor circulation may be helped by Phos. Symptoms are worse in the evening and morning and before or during a thunderstorm. They are also made worse for too much physical activity, hot food and drink and lying on the left side. Symptoms improve in the fresh open air and with lying on the back or right side. They are better after sleep or when the person is touched or stroked. People who need Phos. do not like to be alone when ill and improve with the sympathy and attention of others. They are warm, kind, affectionate people who are highly creative, imaginative and artistic. They enjoy the company of other people and need stimulation to give impetus to their ideas. Phos. people have an optimistic outlook, are full of enthusiasm but sometimes promise much and deliver little. They are very tactile and like to be touched or stroked and offered sympathy when unhappy or unwell. They enjoy a variety of different foods but tend to suffer from digestive upsets. Phos. people are usually tall, slim and may be dark or fair-haired, with an attractive, open appearance. They like to wear brightly coloured clothes and are usually popular. They have a fear of illness, especially cancer, and of dying and also of the dark and supernatural forces. They are apprehensive of water and fear being a failure in their work. Thunderstorms make them nervous.

Pulsatilla nigricans

Pulsatilla, *Anemone pratensis*, meadow anemone

This attractive plant closely resembles *Anemone pulsatilla*, the pasqueflower, which is used in herbal medicine but has smaller flowers. *Anemone pratensis* is a native of Germany, Denmark and Scandinavia and has been used medicinally for hundreds of years. The plant produces beautiful deep purple flowers with orange centres and both leaves and flowers are covered with fine, silky hairs. The whole fresh plant is gathered and made into a pulp, and liquid is extracted to make the homeopathic remedy. It is used to treat a wide variety of disorders with both physical and mental symptoms. It is useful for ailments in which there is a greenish, yellowish discharge. Hence it is used for colds and coughs and sinusitis with the production of profuse catarrh or phlegm. Also, eye infections with discharge such as styes and conjunctivitis. Digestive disorders are helped by it, particularly indigestion, heartburn, nausea and sickness caused by eating too much fatty or rich food. The remedy is helpful for female disorders in which there are a variety of physical and emotional symptoms. These include premenstrual tension, menstrual problems, menopausal symptoms and cystitis, with accompanying symptoms of mood swings, depression and tearfulness. It is a remedy for headaches and migraine, swollen glands, inflammation and pain in the bones and joints as in rheumatic and arthritic disorders, nosebleeds, varicose veins, mumps, measles, toothache, acne, frequent urination and incontinence.

Symptoms are worse at night or when it is hot, and after eating heavy, rich food. Symptoms improve out in the cool fresh air and for gentle exercise such as walking. The person feels better after crying and being treated sympathetically by others. Pulsatilla people are usually women who have a mild, passive nature and are kind, gentle and loving. They are easily moved to tears by the plight of others and love animals and people alike. The person yields easily to the requests and demands of others and is a peacemaker who likes to avoid a scene. An outburst of anger is very much out of character, and a Pulsatilla person usually has many friends. The person likes rich and sweet foods, although these may upset the digestion, and dislikes spicy meals. Pulsatilla people may fear darkness, being left alone, dying and any illness leading to insanity. They are fearful of crowds, the supernatural and tend to be claustrophobic. Usually, they are fair and blue-eyed with clear, delicate skin that blushes readily. They are attractive and slightly overweight or plump.

Rhus toxicodendron

Rhus tox.; *Rhus radicaris*, American poison ivy, poison oak, poison vine.

This large bush or small tree is a native species of the United States and Canada. Its leaves are extremely irritant to the touch, causing an inflamed and painful rash, swelling and ulceration. Often the person experiences malaise, swollen glands, headache, feverishness and a lack of appetite. The plant produces white flowers with a green or yellow tinge in June, followed later by clusters of berries. The fresh leaves are gathered and pulped to make the remedy used in homeopathy. It is used especially as a treatment for skin rashes and lesions with hot, burning sensations and also for inflammation of muscles and joints. Hence it is used to treat eczema, chilblains, cold sores, shingles, nappy rash and other conditions in which there is a dry, scaling or blistered skin. Also, for rheumatism, sciatica, lumbago, gout, synovitis (inflammation of the synovial membranes surrounding joints), osteoarthritis, ligament and tendon strains. Feverish symptoms caused by viral infections, such as high temperature, chills and shivering, swollen, watering eyes, aching joints, nausea and vomiting, may be helped by Rhus tox. Some menstrual problems, including heavy bleeding and abdominal pains that are relieved by lying down, benefit from this remedy. People who are helped by Rhus tox tend to be depressed and miserable when ill, with a tendency to burst into tears, and are highly susceptible to cold, damp weather. Usually they have a dry, irritating cough and thirst and are irritable, anxious and restless. The symptoms are made worse in stormy, wet, windy weather and at night, and when the person moves after a period of rest. Also, for becoming chilled when undressing. Warm, dry conditions and gentle exercise improve and lessen the symptoms. Rhus tox people may be initially shy in company, but when they lose this are charming, entertaining and lively and make friends easily. They are usually conscientious and highly motivated and serious about their work to the extent of being somewhat workaholic. Rhus tox people often have an inner restlessness and become depressed and moody when affected by illness. They may be prone to carry out small compulsive rituals in order to function.

Ruta graveolens

Ruta grav.; rue, garden rue, herbygrass, ave-grace, herb-of-grace, bitter herb

This hardy, evergreen plant is a native of southern Europe but has been cultivated in Britain for centuries, having been first brought here by the Romans. It thrives in poor soil in a dry and partially shaded situation, producing yellow-green flowers. The whole plant has a distinctive, pungent, unpleasant smell and was once used to repel insects, pestilence and infections. It has been used medicinally throughout history to treat ailments in both animals and people, and was used to guard against the plague. It was believed to be effective in guarding against witchcraft, and Hippocrates recommended it as an antidote to poisoning. Rue was believed to have beneficial effects on sight and was used by the great artists, such as Michelangelo, to keep vision sharp. In the Catholic High Mass, brushes made from rue were once used to sprinkle the holy water, hence the name herb-of-grace. Taken internally in large doses, rue has toxic effects causing vomiting, a swollen tongue, fits and delirium.

The homeopathic remedy is prepared from the sap of the green parts of the plant before the flowers open. It is indicated especially for bone and joint injuries and disorders, and those affecting tendons, ligaments and muscles where there is severe, deep, tearing pain. Hence it is used for synovitis (inflammation of the synovial membranes lining joints), rheumatism, sprains, strains, bruising, fractures and dislocations and also sciatica. Also, it is a useful remedy for eye strain with tired, aching eyes, redness and inflammation and headache. Chest problems may be relieved by Ruta grav., particularly painful deep coughs, and some problems affecting the rectum, such as prolapse. Pain and infection in the socket of a tooth after dental extraction may be helped by this remedy. A person who is ill and who benefits from Ruta grav. tends to feel low, anxious, depressed and dissatisfied both with himself (or herself) and others. The symptoms are usually worse in cold, damp weather, for resting and lying down and for exercise out of doors. They improve with heat and gentle movement indoors.

Sepia officinalis

Sepia; ink of the cuttlefish

Cuttlefish ink has been used since ancient times, both for medicinal purposes and as a colour in artists' paint. The cuttlefish has the ability to change colour to blend in with its surroundings and squirts out the dark brown-black ink when threatened by predators. Sepia was known to Roman physicians who used it as a cure for baldness. In homeopathy it is mainly used as an excellent remedy for women experiencing menstrual and menopausal problems. It was investigated and proved by Hahnemann in 1834. It is used to treat premenstrual tension, menstrual pain and heavy bleeding, infrequent or suppressed periods, menopausal symptoms such as hot flushes, and postnatal depression. Physical and emotional symptoms caused by an imbalance of hormones are helped by Sepia. Also, conditions in which there is extreme fatigue or exhaustion with muscular aches and pains. Digestive complaints, including nausea and sickness, abdominal pain and wind, caused by eating dairy products, and headaches with giddiness and nausea are relieved by Sepia. Also, it is a remedy for incontinence, hot, sweaty feet and verrucas (a wart on the foot). A woman often experiences pelvic, dragging pains frequently associated with prolapse of the womb. Disorders of the circulation, especially varicose veins and cold extremities, benefit from sepia.

Symptoms are worse in cold weather, before a thunderstorm, in the late afternoon, evening, early in the morning and also before a period in women and if the person receives sympathy from others. The symptoms are better with heat and warmth, quick vigorous movements, having plenty to do and out in the fresh open air. People suitable for Sepia are usually, but not exclusively, women. They tend to be tall, thin, with a yellowish complexion and are rather self-contained and indifferent to others. Sepia people may become easily cross, especially with family and close friends, and harbour resentment. In company, they make a great effort to appear outgoing and love to dance. A woman may be either an externally hard, successful career person or someone who constantly feels unable to cope, especially with looking after the home and family. Sepia people have strongly held beliefs and cannot stand others taking a contrary opinion. When ill, they hate to be fussed over or have the sympathy of others. They like both sour and sweet foods and alcoholic drinks but are upset by milk products and fatty meals. They harbour deep insecurity and fear being left alone, illness resulting in madness, and loss of their material possessions and wealth. One physical attribute is that they often have a brown mark in the shape of a saddle across the bridge of the nose.

Silicea terra

Silicea; silica

Silica is one of the main rock-forming minerals and is also found in living things, where its main function is to confer strength and resilience. In homeopathy, it is used to treat disorders of the skin, nails and bones and recurring inflammations and infections, especially those that occur because the person is somewhat rundown or has an inadequate diet. Also, some disorders of the nervous system are relieved by Silicea. The homeopathic remedy used to be derived from ground flint or quartz but is now prepared by chemical reaction. The remedy is used for catarrhal infections such as colds, influenza, sinusitis, ear infections including glue ear. Also, for inflammations producing pus, such as a boil, carbuncle, abscess, stye, whitlow (infection of the fingernail) and peritonsillar abscess. It is beneficial in helping the natural expulsion of a foreign body, such as a splinter in the skin. It is a remedy for a headache beginning at the back of the head and radiating forwards over the right eye, and for stress-related conditions of overwork and sleeplessness.

Symptoms are worse for cold, wet weather, especially when clothing is inadequate, draughts, swimming and bathing, becoming chilled after removing clothes and in the morning. They are better for warmth and heat, summer weather, warm clothing, particularly a hat or head covering, and not lying on the left side. People who are suitable for Silicea tend to be thin with a fine build and pale skin. They often have thin straight hair. They are prone to dry, cracked skin and nails and may suffer from skin infections. Silicea people are usually unassuming, and lacking in confidence and physical stamina. They are conscientious and hard-working to the point of working too hard once a task has been undertaken. However, they may hesitate to commit themselves through lack of confidence and fear of responsibility. Silicea people are tidy and obsessive about small details. They may feel 'put upon' but lack the courage to speak out, and may take this out on others who are not responsible for the situation. They fear failure and dislike exercise because of physical weakness, often feeling mentally and physically exhausted. They enjoy cold foods and drinks.

Sulphur

Sulphur, flowers of sulphur, brimstone

Sulphur has a long history of use in medicine going back to ancient times. Sulphur gives off sulphur dioxide when burnt, which smells unpleasant ('rotten eggs' odour) but acts as a disinfectant. This was used in mediaeval times to limit the spread of infectious diseases. Sulphur is deposited around the edges of hot springs and geysers and where there is volcanic activity. Flowers of sulphur, which is a bright yellow powder, is obtained from the natural mineral deposit and is used to make the homeopathic remedy. Sulphur is found naturally in all body tissues, and in both orthodox medicine and homeopathy is used to treat skin disorders. It is a useful remedy for dermatitis, eczema, psoriasis and a dry, flaky, itchy skin or scalp. Some digestive disorders benefit from it, especially a tendency for food to rise back up to the mouth and indigestion caused by drinking milk. Sulphur is helpful in the treatment of haemorrhoids, premenstrual and menopausal symptoms, eye inflammations such as conjunctivitis, pain in the lower part of the back, catarrhal colds and coughs, migraine headaches and feverish symptoms. Some mental symptoms are helped by this remedy, particularly those brought about by stress or worry, including depression, irritability, insomnia and lethargy. When ill, people who benefit from sulphur feel thirsty rather than hungry and are upset by unpleasant smells. The person soon becomes exhausted and usually sleeps poorly at night and is tired through the day. The symptoms are worse in cold, damp conditions, in the middle of the morning around 11 a.m., and in stuffy, hot, airless rooms. Also, for becoming too hot at night in bed and for wearing too many layers of clothes. Long periods of standing and sitting aggravate the symptoms, and they are worse if the person drinks alcohol or has a wash. Symptoms improve in dry, clear, warm weather and for taking exercise. They are better if the person lies on the right side.

Sulphur people tend to look rather untidy and have dry, flaky skin and coarse, rough hair. They may be thin, round-shouldered and inclined to slouch or be overweight, round and red-faced. Sulphur people have lively, intelligent minds full of schemes and inventions, but are often useless on a practical level. They may be somewhat self-centred with a need to be praised, and fussy over small unimportant details. They enjoy intellectual discussion on subjects that they find interesting and may become quite heated although the anger soon subsides. Sulphur people are often warm and generous with their time and money. They enjoy a wide range of foods but are upset by milk and eggs. They have a fear of being a failure in their work, of heights and the supernatural.

Tarentula cubensis

Tarentula cub.; Cuban tarantula

The bite of the Cuban tarantula spider produces a delayed

response in the victim. About 24 hours after a bite, the site becomes inflamed and red, and swelling, fever and abscess follow. The homeopathic remedy, made from the poison of the spider, is used to treat similar septic conditions, such as an abscess, boil, carbuncle or whitlow (an infection of the fingernail) and genital itching. Also, it is a remedy for anthrax and shock, and is of value as a last-resort treatment in severe conditions. The infected areas are often tinged blue, and there may be burning sensations of pain that are especially severe at night. It is of particular value in the treatment of recurring boils or carbuncles. The symptoms tend to improve with smoking and are made worse by physical activity and consuming cold drinks.

Thuja occidentalis

Thuja; tree of life, yellow cedar, arbor vitae, false white cedar

This coniferous, evergreen tree is a native species of the northern United States and Canada and grows to a height of about 30 feet. It has feathery green leaves with a strong, aromatic smell resembling that of camphor. The leaves and twigs were used by the Indian peoples to treat a variety of infections and disorders, and the plant has long been used in herbal medicine. It is an important remedy in aromatherapy. The fresh green leaves and twigs are used to prepare the homeopathic remedy, which is especially valuable in the treatment of warts and wartlike tumours on any part of the body. It is a useful remedy for shingles and also has an effect on the genital and urinary tracts. Hence it is used to treat inflammations and infections such as cystitis and urethritis and also pain on ovulation. It may be given as a remedy for infections of the mouth, teeth and gums, catarrh and for tension headaches.

People who benefit from Thuja tend to sweat profusely, and it helps to alleviate this symptom. They tend to suffer from insomnia and when they do manage to sleep, may talk or cry out. They are prone to severe left-sided frontal headaches that may be present on waking in the morning. Symptoms are worse at night, from being too hot in bed and after breakfast. Also, at 3 a.m. and 3 p.m. and in weather that is cold and wet. Symptoms are felt more severely on the left side. Symptoms improve for movement and stretching of the limbs, massage and after sweating. People suitable for Thuja tend to be insecure and unsure about themselves. They try hard to please others but are very sensitive to criticism and soon become depressed. This may lead them to neglect their appearance. Thuja people are often thin and pale and tend to have greasy skin and perspire easily.

Urtica urens

Urtica; stinging nettle

One of the few plants that is familiar to all and that, for

hundreds of years, has been valued for its medicinal and culinary uses. Nettles have always been used as a source of food both for people and animals, the young leaves being a nutritious vegetable with a high content of vitamin C. Nettles were thought to purify the blood, and an ancient cure for rheumatism and muscular weakness was the practice of 'urtication', or lashing the body with stinging nettles. The hairs covering the leaves of the nettle release a volatile liquid when touched, which causes the familiar skin reaction of painful, white bumps to appear. The fresh, green parts of the plant are used to prepare the homeopathic remedy, which is used as a treatment for burning and stinging of the skin. Hence it is used to treat allergic reactions of the skin, urticaria, or nettle rash, insect bites and stings and skin lesions caused by burns and scalds. Also, for eczema, chicken pox, nerve inflammation and pain (neuritis and neuralgia), shingles, rheumatism, gout and cystitis in which there are burning, stinging pains. The person who benefits from this remedy is prone to inflamed, itching and irritated skin complaints and may be fretful, impatient and restless. Symptoms are made worse by touch, cold, wet weather, snow and contact with water. Allergic skin reactions may occur if the person eats shellfish such as prawns. The symptoms improve if the affected skin is rubbed and also if the person rests and lies down.

Minor Homeopathic Remedies

Aethusa cynapium

Aethusa; fool's parsley, dog parsley, dog poison, lesser hemlock

This plant is a common weed that grows throughout most of Europe, including Great Britain. It resembles hemlock but is smaller and has three to five long, thin, leaflike bands that hang down beneath each flower head of small, white flowers. The leaves have an unpleasant smell although this is less strong than that of hemlock and is quite different from that of garden parsley. The plant is poisonous, although less potent than hemlock, and has effects on the digestive organs and nervous system. The green parts of the flowering plant are used in homeopathy, and it is used especially to treat bouts of violent vomiting, particularly in babies with an allergy to milk. Accompanying symptoms include abdominal pains and diarrhoea. It is used to treat summer diarrhoea in children and also severe mental symptoms of confusion, fits and delirium. (These symptoms are produced in cases of poisoning with fool's parsley). It is used to help alleviate mental weakness and fatigue and inability to concentrate. Symptoms are made worse by heat, summer weather, and in the evening and between 3 and 4 a.m. in the early morning. They improve out in the fresh open air and when the person has the company of others.

Agaricus muscarius

Agaricus; *Amanita muscaria*, common toadstool, fly agaric, bug agaric

This striking toadstool, with its bright red-orange cap studded with small white flakes, grows in damp, boggy, upland woods in Scotland, northern Europe, North America and Asia. It is deadly poisonous, and juice obtained from the fungus used to be extracted and used as a fly killer. It has effects on the mind and has been exploited for its hallucinogenic properties. These attributes mean that it must be handled with very great care and its use is banned in some countries. The whole fresh fungus is used to prepare the homeopathic remedy, which is given for chilblains and itching, burning hot, swollen fingers and toes. Also, it is a remedy for epilepsy and disorders in which there are twitching, jerking spasms of muscles (chorea). It is given as a remedy for dizziness and unsteadiness, confusion, delirium tremens (alcoholism) and senile dementia. People who benefit from it feel the cold at all times but particularly acutely when not well. Symptoms are made worse by cold conditions or weather, thunderstorms and after a meal. They improve with gentle, slow movements.

Ailanthus olandulosa

Ailanthus; *Ailanthus altissima*, shade tree, Chinese sumach, copal tree, tree of heaven, tree of the gods, ailanto

A large, attractive tree that produces yellow-green flowers with a highly unpleasant smell. When inhaled, the scent causes digestive upset, and the fresh flowers are used to make the homeopathic remedy. The tree is a native of China but was introduced into Britain during the 18th century as an ornamental species. It is used as a remedy for glandular fever in which there is a highly painful sore throat and swollen glands. The tonsils are red and inflamed and it is difficult to swallow. The person may have a severe headache and pains in the muscles. The symptoms are made worse by swallowing and bending the body forwards. Also, for lying down and during the morning, and for being exposed to light.

Aloe socotrina

Aloe; *Aloe ferox*, the common aloe

Aloes are succulent plants, and there are a number of species flourishing in the hotter climates of the world. Juice drained from the cut leaves is dried and made into a resin that is powdered to make the homeopathic remedy. Aloe has been used in medicine for many centuries and was given by Greek and Roman physicians for digestive and abdominal disorders. In more recent times, it has been used as a medicine to purge the bowels.

Aloe was investigated and proved by Dr Constantine Hering in the mid-1800s, and the remedy is used in homeopathy for various congestive problems. These include headache, enlarged prostate gland in men, prolapsed uterus, haemorrhoids, or piles, diarrhoea and constipation and overindulgence in alcoholic drinks. Symptoms are made worse by heat and hot, dry summer weather. They are at their most severe in the very early morning and following meals and drinks. Symptoms improve in cold weather and for cold applications, and also for abdominal flatulence. People who are suitable for Aloe tend to be short-tempered and cross, feeling generally displeased with themselves and those around them. They frequently feel tired and unable to face up to their daily work, and symptoms are at their most severe when the person is constipated. Aloe types enjoy beer but it upsets their digestion.

Aluminium oxide

Alumina; oxide of aluminium

Aluminium is obtained from bauxite, a type of rock containing hydrated aluminium oxide. In conventional medicine, aluminium is used in indigestion remedies where there is an excess of stomach acid. The brain tissue of people suffering from Alzheimer's disease has been found to contain elevated levels of aluminium, and there is some concern that the metal may leach out from cooking utensils, especially when acid fruits are stewed. One of the main uses of the homeopathic remedy is for the treatment of confusional states. It is also used to treat all ailments where there is a slowness or sluggishness in the system. The remedy is given for senile dementia, confusion and memory loss, constipation, poor co-ordination, and heaviness and deadness of the limbs, poor flow of urine, and giddiness when the eyes are closed. Symptoms are worse in the morning and for being out in the cold and also following meals that are high in carbohydrate and salt. People suitable for alumina are usually pale and thin with dry skin. They are pessimistic and gloomy, beset with feelings of impending disaster, and have a phobia about sharp, pointed objects such as knives. Alumina types may experience strange cravings for inappropriate substances to eat, but they do not like meat or beer.

Ammonium carbonicum

Ammon. carb.; ammonium carbonate, sal volatile

Ammonium carbonate was long in use in medicine in the treatment of scarlet fever and as a constituent of smelling salts. The remedy was investigated and proved by Hahnemann in the 1800s and was found to be an effective treatment for a number of different disorders. The remedy is obtained from a chemical reaction between ammonium chloride and sodium carbonate. It is of particular value if the circulation is slow and if the heart is weak. It can be used to treat post-viral tiredness and ME (myalgic encephalomyelitis). The symptoms are made worse by prolonged exertion and cloudy, overcast weather. They improve in warm, dry weather and surroundings, by lying down with the feet higher than the head and by the application of pressure. People suitable for Ammon. carb. are usually of large build and soon feel tired. They tend to be short-tempered, irritable and are prone to forgetfulness and bouts of crying. They are especially sensitive to the effects of overcast, dull weather.

Ammonium muriaticum

Ammon. mur.; sal ammoniac, ammonium chloride

Ammonium chloride has been used since ancient times and was especially prized by alchemists. There used to be only one source of the substance, which was the Fire Mountain in central Asia, but it is now prepared by chemical reaction. Ammonium chloride is used in conventional medicine in remedies for colds and coughs, and it has several important industrial uses. It is a remedy for conditions in which there is a feeling of tightness and constriction. Ailments include coughs, bronchitis and pneumonia in which it feels as though there is a tight band around the chest, and there is a sticky, thick mucus. Also for disorders affecting joints and tendons, backache, lumbago and sciatica with symptoms especially affecting the left side and being worse in the morning. Often the person experiences a frontal headache at the base of the nose and may have an irritated dry scalp and dandruff. Symptoms are worse in the early hours of the morning between 2 and 4 a.m. and also during the afternoon. They are better in the evening and night and improve for brisk exercise, especially out in the fresh air. The person who benefits from Ammon. mur. tends to be obese, although the limbs may appear to be thin, and has a puffy skin because of fluid retention. The metabolism is slow, and the circulation is sluggish and erratic, which may cause pains of a throbbing nature. Ammon. mur. people have a somewhat pessimistic outlook on life and cry easily, and tend to have a painful heel that may be caused by an ulcer. They may take an unreasonable dislike of some people and are afraid of the dark.

Amyl nitrosum

Amyl nitrate

This remedy is used for irregularities of heartbeat and anxiety. Symptoms include a racing heart (tachycardia), throbbing in the head and awareness of the heart rate with the sensation of the heart missing a beat and palpitations. There may be pain and numbness in the chest, which can spread to involve the arm and may be severe, as in angina. The person may experience hot flushes and sweats, especially if a woman going through the menopause. There is a feeling of fullness in the head and the person may flush easily.

Anacardium orientale

Anacard. or.; *Semecarpus anacardium*, cashew nut, marking nut

There are several products of the cashew nut tree that are useful to humans, and these have long been used for culinary and medicinal purposes. The nuts are gathered and eaten and used in cookery, and the fruits also are edible. The nut is surrounded by an inner and outer shell, and in between the two there is a thick, caustic, dark fluid that is the substance used in homeopathy. This fluid causes blistering of the skin and has been used to treat warts, ulcers, corns, bunions and other lesions of the skin. The fluid was also used to make an indelible ink by mixing it with chalk, and this was employed to mark cloth (hence 'marking nut'). Arabian physicians used the juice for treating psychiatric and nervous system disorders, including convulsions, paralysis and dementia. The cashew nut tree has an attractive appearance, produces perfumed pink flowers, and is a native species of the East Indies and Asia. In homeopathy, the remedy is used to treat symptoms of constriction, as though there are tight belts around the body. The person feels as though the digestive system is blocked by a plug, and there is pain, indigestion and constipation. Also, Anacard. or. is given for rheumatism and ulcers, and while symptoms are initially relieved by eating, they are worse once digestion is completed. Symptoms are worse late at night around midnight and for pressure and hot baths. They are relieved by fasting. People suitable for this remedy tend to be totally lacking in self-confidence, feeling constantly inferior. They often have a poor memory and may be prone to mental disorders, particularly an inability to distinguish between reality and fantasy.

Antimonium tartaricum

Antim. tart.; tartar emetic, antimony potassium tartrate

This substance is important in the manufacture of textiles, being used to fix dyes used to colour materials. In orthodox medicine it has been used in cough remedies and as an emetic to cause vomiting. The homeopathic remedy is obtained by means of a chemical reaction between potassium tartrate and antimony oxide. It is used in the treatment of bronchitis and conditions in which there is an accumulation of phlegm. Breathing is difficult and laboured, and the person has a wheezing cough that is ineffective in bringing up the accumulated fluid. It is useful for young children and elderly persons who are in a weakened condition and are not able to cough effectively. Also, it may be used as a remedy for a tension headache with a feeling of tight constriction around the head. The person generally does not feel thirsty and may have some puffiness of the skin because of fluid retention. The tongue appears to be thickly furred. Symptoms are made worse by exercise, lying flat, wet, cold conditions and in warm, stuffy, airless rooms. They are relieved by cold, dry air and resting by sitting propped up.

Apomorphia

Alkaloid of morphine

This is a remedy for severe and persistent vomiting accompanied by weakness, dizziness, fainting and sweating. Nausea may or may not be present. The vomiting may be the result of a number of different causes, such as the morning sickness of pregnancy. Additionally, it may be caused by overindulgence in alcohol or too much rich food or misuse of drugs.

Aranea diadema

Aranea diad.; *Aranea diadematus*, papal cross spider

This spider is widely found in many countries throughout the northern hemisphere. It has a spherical brown body marked with white spots on its back that form the shape of a crucifix. It is a web-spinning spider that paralyses its prey by biting and injecting a venom. The whole spider is used to prepare the homeopathic remedy, which was first investigated and proved by von Grauvogl, a German doctor during the mid 1800s. He used it as a remedy for symptoms of cutting and burning neuralgic pains that are made worse by damp, cold conditions. It is used to treat any kind of neuralgic pains but especially those affecting the face. The pains usually arise suddenly and are intermittent and severe in nature, being hot and searing. There may also be sensations of numbness and symptoms are worsened by exposure to cold, damp conditions and any cold applications. They improve in warm, summer weather and with warm applications. Also, and most unusually, they are relieved by smoking.

Argentum metallicum

Argent. met.; silver

Silver is usually found in association with other metallic minerals in ore deposits in ancient rocks. It has been prized throughout human history and used to make jewellery, utensils, artistic ornamentation and has modern industrial uses, e.g. in photographic film. It is widely used in dentistry in fillings and is valued in conventional medicine for its antiseptic and astringent properties. The homeopathic remedy is used for arthritic and rheumatic disorders, particularly those affecting the joints of the toes, ankles, fingers and wrists. The joints are painful, but usually the pain is intermittent in character and may disappear altogether for a time. Other types of pain from deep within the body may also be relieved by Argent. met. and also asthmatic and bronchitic symptoms and laryngitis. Symptoms are made worse for movement of the affected joints and also late in the morning towards midday. They improve with resting the affected part and being out in fresh clean air. Symptoms are better at night and for the application of gentle pressure.

Arsenicum iodatum

Arsen. iod.; iodide of arsenic

This homeopathic remedy is obtained from a chemical reaction between iodine and metallic arsenic and was formerly used in the treatment of tuberculosis. It is used as a remedy for allergic conditions such as hay fever in which there is a copious watery discharge from the nose. Also, for bronchitis, psoriasis and eczema and hyperactivity in children. The symptoms are worse at night around midnight and are better if the person is out in the fresh, cool air.

Arum triphyllum

Arum triph.; jack-in-the-pulpit, Indian turnip, wild turnip, pepper turnip, dragon root, memory root

This is a common wild plant of North America and Canada, which has unusually shaped leaves that are borne on long stalks. It has a broad, flattened root that is highly irritant if eaten, causing severe symptoms of vomiting, nausea and diarrhoea and burning inflammation of the mucous membranes of the mouth and digestive tract. ('Arum' is derived from the Arabic word for 'fire', *ar*). The fresh root is used to make the homeopathic remedy, which is used as a remedy for colds and hay fever with symptoms mainly on the left side. There may be cracking and bleeding of the skin around the nose and mouth and dry, sore lips. It is also given for hoarseness and laryngitis. Typically, there is a burning and profuse nasal discharge, and the person may feel hot and unwell. The symptoms may be caused by overuse of the voice, for instance if the person is a singer, or be brought on by exposure to the cold. Symptoms are made worse by cold weather, especially if exposed to biting winds, and also by lying down. They improve for drinking coffee and are also better in the morning.

Asafoetida

Ferula foetida, food of the gods, devil's dung

Ferula foetida is a large plant that is a native of eastern Iran and Afghanistan, and grows to a height of several feet. It has a thick and fleshy root, and when this is cut, a white, gumlike, milky fluid is exuded that hardens into resin. The sap of the plant smells rank and unpleasant and has an effect upon the digestive system. The hardened gum is made into a powder for use in homeopathy, and it is used for digestive disorders and hysteria. It is a remedy for indigestion, abdominal pains and flatulence, bloatedness and hysterical symptoms.

Astacus fluviatilis

Crawfish

This homeopathic remedy is used to treat allergic skin reactions that may have arisen as a result of eating shellfish. There is a raised, itchy skin rash (urticaria) and there may be a high temperature, malaise, chills and swollen glands. Symptoms are made worse by exposure to cold and draughts.

Avena sativa

Avena; wild oats

Oats have been cultivated for centuries as a nutritious source of food for both people and livestock. Oats are the only known food to reduce the level of cholesterol in the blood. The fresh green parts of the plant are used to make the homeopathic remedy, and in both homeopathy and herbal medicine the preparations are used to treat nervous complaints. The homeopathic remedy is given as a treatment for nervous exhaustion, stress, sleeplessness and anxiety. It helps to relieve the nervous symptoms of those suffering from alcohol abuse and may be used to treat impotence. Symptoms are made worse by consumption of alcohol and relieved by a good night's sleep.

Baptisia tinctoria

Baptisia; wild indigo, indigo weed, horsefly weed, rattlebush

This is an herbaceous, perennial plant that grows throughout Canada and most of the United States in dry, upland, wooded habitats. It has a dark woody root that is pale on the inside with many small roots arising from it, and this is the part used in homeopathy. The root was ground down and used by the Indian peoples both as a medicine and as a dye. ('Baptisia' is derived from the Greek word *bapto*, meaning 'to dye'). The plant grows to about three feet in height, producing yellow flowers in August and September. It is poisonous if eaten in large quantities but preparations of the root are valued for their antibacterial, antiseptic, astringent properties. In homeopathy it is used to treat acute, severe infections and fevers. These include influenza, whooping cough, scarlet fever and typhoid fever. The person feels unwell and may be exhausted, confused and delirious with a discoloured tongue and bad breath. There may be diarrhoea with an offensive smell. Symptoms are made worse by hot, humid airless conditions and improve with gentle exercise in the fresh, open air, once the person is convalescent.

Baryta carbonica

Baryta carb., witherite, barium carbonate

The barium carbonate that is used to make the homeopathic remedy is found as white crystals of witherite and barite in ancient rocks. Barium, which is derived from these minerals, is used in radiology and also in the manufacture of glassware. Witherite was once used medicinally to treat swollen glands and tuberculosis. In homeopathy it is a useful remedy for children and elderly persons suffering from intellectual and, possibly, physical impairment. Children may have Down's syndrome or similar disorders, and often have a disproportionately large head and impairment of growth. They tend to suffer from recurrent respiratory infections such as tonsillitis. Elderly persons who benefit from Baryta carb. may suffer from dementia or be physically and intellectually impaired because of an event such as a stroke. People suitable for this remedy are shy and unsure of themselves and they need a great deal of reassurance. They tend to be childlike, and need to be guided into making the right decisions. Symptoms are made worse by cold in any form, especially damp and chilly weather and biting cold winds. They improve with warmth in any form and with exercise in the open air. The person feels better if warm clothing is worn.

Bellis perennis

Bellis; the daisy, bruisewort, garden or common daisy

This little plant with its dark green leaves and white flowers with yellow centres, is so common as to be familiar to all. The leaves contain an acrid liquid that protects the plant from being eaten by insects or grazing animals. The daisy has a long history of medicinal use, having been used since mediaeval times to relieve bruising (hence bruisewort). The whole fresh flowering plant is used to make the homeopathic remedy, which is mainly used to treat bruising, pain and inflammation following accidental injury, trauma or surgery. It is useful for the prevention of infection and in the treatment of boils and abscesses. Symptoms are more severe if the person becomes chilled when already too hot, and glands may be swollen. Arms and legs may feel cold or numb. Bellis may be given during pregnancy to relieve pains and cramps. Symptoms are made worse by chilling, becoming wet and for sweating and being too hot at night in bed. They improve with massage or rubbing of the painful area and for gentle exercise and movement.

Benzoicum acidum

Benz. ac.; benzoic acid

Benzoic acid is found naturally in a resinous substance, benzoin gum, that occurs in some plants. A combination of sodium and benzoic acid forms sodium benzoate, which is used in the preservation of food. The homeopathic remedy is used for arthritic conditions and gout and also for urinary disorders, particularly kidney stones. There is a characteristic clicking of the joints in arthritic conditions and severe, searing pain. Urinary complaints are accompanied by the production of a dark urine that smells offensive and associated pain. The person is very sensitive to cold and often feels chilled. Benz. ac. may also be given as a treatment for menstrual disorders and a prolapsed uterus. Symptoms are made worse for getting cold while undressing or chilling because of winter weather or draughts. They improve with heat and hot applications to the painful part.

Berberis vulgaris

Berberis, barberry, pipperidge bush

Berberis is a common bushy shrub that grows throughout Europe, producing pale green leaves, yellow flowers and glossy red berries. The berries have always been valued for culinary purposes, and the plant also has a long history of medicinal use. The physicians of ancient Greece and Arabia used Berberis to treat feverish conditions, haemorrhage, gastroenteritis, dysentery and jaundice. In herbal medicine it is still used to treat jaundice, liver disorders, gallstones and digestive disorders. The fresh root of the plant is used to prepare the homeopathic remedy, which is used in the treatment of kidney complaints accompanied by severe pain, such as renal colic and kidney stones. These complaints may be accompanied by the production of dark-coloured abnormal urine with an offensive odour. Also, it is used for gallstones, jaundice and biliary colic accompanied by the passing of pale faeces. People suitable for this remedy tend to have an unhealthy appearance, being pale with sunken features and dark shadows beneath the eyes. Symptoms may show rapid fluctuations and are made worse by prolonged standing. They are relieved for stretching exercise and gentle movements.

Borax

Borate of sodium

This homeopathic remedy acts on the gastro-intestinal tract and is used in the treatment of digestive disorders. It is particularly helpful as a remedy for pains, diarrhoea, nausea and vomiting. These may be accompanied by sweating, fever and giddiness. Symptoms are made worse by downward movements such as sitting or lying down.

Bothrops lanceolatus

Bothrops; *Lachesis lanceolatus*, fer-de-lance, yellow pit viper

This greyish-brown snake, marked with a diamond pattern, is a native animal of the Caribbean island of

Martinique. It produces a deadly venom, and if a person receives a bite, the affected part swells and eventually becomes affected by gangrene. The venom of the snake is harvested and used to make the homeopathic remedy, which is given for conditions of the blood such as haemorrhage and thrombosis. It is also used for strokes that affect the left side of the brain, producing symptoms of weakness and paralysis on the right side of the body and speech difficulty. People who need Bothrops are frequently exhausted, with slow, weary movements, and may be subject to tremor (involuntary trembling).

Bovista

Lycoperdon bovista; warted puffball, *Lycoperdon giganteum*

This fungus can be found in countries throughout Europe and has the shape of a round, white ball, varying in diameter from four inches to one foot. When the fungus is ripe, an irregular gash forms in its surface and dark browny/green spores are released. Young puffballs are eaten in some countries and they have a long history of use among country dwellers. The puffball was cut and applied to wounds to staunch bleeding and also burnt to produce a smoke that would stupefy bees so that honey could be collected from a hive. In homeopathy, the remedy is used for speech disorders such as stammering and also for skin lesions, including eczema, blisters, warts, bunions, corns and nettle rash. These skin eruptions tend to weep and crust over and produce severe itching. Symptoms are made worse by heat and relieved by cold applications.

Bufo rana

Bufo, the common toad

This toad is found in many countries throughout the world and has a mottled brown and pale warty skin. When the toad is disturbed and feels threatened, it secretes a toxic irritant substance from pores in its skin, especially from the raised pouches above its eyes. This poisonous substance is noxious and prevents the toad from being eaten. It affects the mucous membranes of the mouth, throat, eyes, etc, and can produce quite severe symptoms, even in larger predators that might be tempted to attack the toad. The poison has a long history of use in Chinese medicine and is collected and prepared to make the homeopathic remedy, which was first investigated and proved by the American homeopath Dr James Tyler Kent. It is used to treat epilepsy, in which the person is disturbed by bright lights or music before the onset of a fit and moves the tongue rapidly (lapping). After the fit, the sufferer is left with a severe headache. Symptoms are made worse at night and for sleep and during menstruation in women. They are much better in the morning and after resting lying down. People who benefit from this remedy have a puffy appearance because of fluid retention. They are apt to lose their temper if unable to make their views understood.

Cactus grandiflorus

Cactus grand; *Selinecereus grandiflorus*, night-blooming cereus, sweet-scented cactus, vanilla cactus, large-flowered cactus

This plant grows in the parched, arid desert regions of South America, Mexico and the United States. It is a shrubby plant with thick fleshy stems and large white flowers with yellow centres. The flowers are about eight to twelve inches across and have a pleasant perfume resembling vanilla. They open in the evening and are closed during the day. The homeopathic remedy is made from the fresh flowers and young stems, and it was investigated and proved in 1862 by Dr Rubins. He discovered that it produced effects on the heart with feelings of constriction and pain. Hence, the remedy is used to treat the unpleasant and frightening symptoms of angina. These include severe, gripping pain that is worse for physical exertion and stress, and a feeling of the chest being held and compressed by tight, constricting bands. There may be numbness, coldness and tingling in the left hand and arm and palpitations. The person feels extremely anxious and fears that death is imminent, and the pain is worse if he or she lies on the left side. Symptoms are worse from late morning until late evening and improve for lying on the right side with the head raised. A person with these symptoms needs reassurance and should not be left alone.

Calcarea hypophosphorosa

Hypophosphate of lime

This is a remedy for persons with the Calcarea constitutional type. The remedy is used for arthritic and rheumatic disorders, especially of the hands and wrists. The hands feel clammy and cold, and the symptoms are made worse by cold, damp weather. The person is very susceptible to cold and has a pale, chilly skin.

Calcarea iodata

Iodide of lime

A remedy for glandular swellings and infections in the neck, including tonsillitis, swollen adenoids and enlarged thyroid (goitre). It is also given for fibroids in the uterus and similar benign breast lumps of a fibrous nature.

Calcarea sulphurica

Calc. sulph.; calcium sulphate, plaster of Paris, gypsum

The source of calcium sulphate is the mineral deposit gypsum, which was formed as a precipitate when salt water evaporated. It is one of the SCHUSSLER TISSUE SALTS (*see*

Glossary) and is used to make plaster casts for immobilising fractured bones. It is a remedy for infected conditions of the skin in which pus is produced. Ailments include boils, carbuncles, skin ulcers and abscesses and infected eczema. The skin looks grey and unhealthy and feels cold and clammy although the soles of the feet may be hot. There may be yellow fur on the tongue, and the person may suffer from malaise and weakness. Symptoms are worse in weather that is wet and cold and improve in dry, fresh open air. They are also better for eating and for drinks of tea. A person suitable for Calc. sulph. has a tendency to be irritable and gloomy, with a jealous nature. Although symptoms are made worse by cold, Calc. sulph. people dislike heat and prefer to feel cool even to the extent of wearing inadequate clothing in winter weather.

Camphora

Camphor; *Laurus camphora*, gum camphor, laurel camphor

This remedy was investigated and proved by Hahnemann who used it to treat a cholera outbreak during the 1830s. The remedy was used again during a further epidemic in 1854 and proved to be highly successful on both occasions. Camphor is obtained from a tree that grows in central China and Japan. Chips of wood are heated with steam, and a liquid is collected from which clear deposits of camphor are precipitated out. Camphor has a characteristic pungent odour and has a range of applications in herbal medicine. In homeopathy, it is used to treat acute conditions and fevers in which there is sweating, a cold clammy pale skin, chills and anxiety. There may be severe symptoms of very low blood pressure, collapse and convulsions. It is sometimes used in circumstances in which other homeopathic remedies have failed to produce an improvement.

Capsicum frutescens

Capsicum; African pepper, red cayenne pepper, chilli pepper, bird pepper

The capsicum plant is a native of South America, West Indies and East Indies, but it is cultivated in many countries throughout the world. Elongated red chilli fruits, which may be used fresh or dried, are much used in Eastern cookery for their fiery properties. They cause sweating and a feeling of heat, dilate blood vessels and promote blood flow. They have been used to treat infectious disorders but are now mainly given for digestive symptoms. Cayenne is one of the most important remedies in herbal practice and is a constituent of many compound medicines. The fruits and seeds are used to prepare the homeopathic remedy, which is used to treat ailments with hot, burning, stinging pains. It is used for indigestion, especially heartburn, piles, or haemorrhoids, diarrhoea, sore throat with painful burning sensation on swallowing, and rheumatic disorders. Symptoms are made worse by cool, draughty conditions and when the person first begins movement. They are made better for warmth and heat, and with sustained exercise and movement. People suitable for this remedy are often fair-haired and blue-eyed and tend to be obese. They are often unfit, disliking physical exercise. Overindulgence in alcohol or rich spicy foods makes them lazy and lethargic, and they tend to have a melancholy disposition. If they go away from home, they soon become depressed and homesick.

Carboneum sulphuratum

Carbon bisulphide

This remedy is used for ailments affecting the nerves, in which there may be weakness, numbness, tremor or paralysis. Also, for some disorders of the eye and vision and for indigestion, abdominal pains, wind, diarrhoea and constipation.

Caulophyllum thalictroides

Caulophyllum; papoose root, squawroot, blueberry root, blue cohosh

This is an attractive perennial plant that is a native species of Canada and North America, growing in moist conditions near creeks or in swamps. It produces greenish-yellow flowers in early summer and, later, large pea-sized seeds that were gathered, roasted and used by the Indian people to make a hot drink. The root of the plant is brown, gnarled and contorted, and this is the part that is used in homeopathy. The preparation made from the root acts as a stimulant on the uterus, and this property was well known to the Indian people, who used the medicine to hasten a slow or painful labour. Caulophyllum was investigated and proved by an American homeopathic doctor, Dr Hale, in the late 1800s, and one of its main uses in homeopathy is to speed up and strengthen weak or painful ineffective contractions of the womb during labour. It is also used to treat absent menstruation and some other conditions of the uterus, such as menstrual and postpartum pain. Caulophyllum is an effective remedy for rheumatic disorders affecting the fingers, hands, wrists, toes, ankles and feet. Typically there are cramp-like stabbing pains that are intermittent in character. Symptoms are worse in women when menstruation is absent or erratic and during pregnancy. All symptoms improve in warm conditions or with the application of heat.

Causticum hahnemanni

Causticum, potassium hydrate

This remedy was prepared, investigated and proved in

the early 1800s by Hahnemann, and is used only in homeopathy. It is prepared by a chemical process in which lime that has been newly burnt is combined with potassium bisulphate in water. The mixture is heated and distilled, and the clear liquid distillate is collected and used to prepare the homeopathic remedy. It is used for weakness of nerves and muscles that control the throat and voice box or vocal cords, bladder, eyelids and face on the right side. Typical throat complaints include hoarseness and loss of the voice and there may be a dry, unproductive cough. Bladder complaints include stress incontinence (i.e. a leakage of urine when the person coughs, sneezes, laughs loudly, etc) and wetting the bed, particularly if suffering from a chill. Other symptoms include sore, hot pains as in heartburn and rheumatic complaints. The symptoms are made worse by exposure to cold winds, physical exercise and also during the evening. They improve with warmth and are better for drinking something cold and having a wash. People suitable for Causticum are often thin, pale and with dark eyes and hair. They are able to enter into other people's suffering and feel the effects of grief very profoundly. They tend to feel the cold rather acutely and may be prone to warts on the skin. Causticum people may be rather rigid in their views and tend to have a weak constitution.

Ceanothus americanus

Ceanothus; red root, Jersey tea root, New Jersey tea, wild snowball

This shrub, which grows to a height of about five feet, is a native species of North America and Canada. It produces numerous small white flowers in June and July, and its leaves were used to make tea during the War of Independence when real tea was hard to come by. The plant has thick, reddish-coloured roots that give it one of its common names. The root is used in herbal medicine, but in homeopathy the fresh leaves, gathered when the plant is in flower, are used to prepare the remedy. Ceanothus is given for abdominal pains and enlargement of the spleen and for symptoms on the left side of the abdomen. The pain is of a piercing nature and is made worse by lying on the left side. Exercise and movement exacerbate the symptoms, but they are relieved by rest and lying still. People who benefit from Ceanothus are extremely sensitive to the cold and like to sit as close as possible to a heat source in order to keep warm.

Chelidonium majus

Chelidonium, greater celandine, wartweed, garden celandine

This plant is a native of many countries in Europe and belongs to the same family as the poppy. The plant has a slender branching stem, large leaves that are a yellow-green colour on their upper surface and grey underneath, and yellow flowers. After flowering, long thin pods are produced containing black seeds. The plant produces a yellowish orange poisonous sap that is acrid, caustic and irritant with an unpleasant smell. The fresh flowering plant is used to prepare the homeopathic remedy, which is mainly used to treat liver and gall bladder disorders. The types of disorder treated include gallstones, hepatitis, abdominal pain and indigestion. There may be symptoms of nausea, jaundice, vomiting and digestive upset with an aching pain located under the right shoulder blade. All symptoms are more common on the right side and are made worse by a change in the weather, for heat, in the afternoon around 4 p.m. and in the early morning around 4 a.m. They are improved by eating, if firm pressure is applied to the painful area, by drinking hot beverages or milk and by passing stools.

People suitable for Chelidonium are often fair-haired and thin with yellowish or sallow skin. They tend to be gloomy and seldom look on the bright side of life and dislike intellectual effort. They are prone to headaches that make them feel heavy and lethargic. Chelidonium types enjoy hot drinks and cheese and may have one hot and one cold foot.

The Chelidonium remedy is also applied externally to

remove warts, and this property has given the plant one of its common names, wartweed.

Cicuta virosa

Cicuta; water hemlock

This plant is a native species of Canada, North America, Siberia and some parts of Europe. It has highly poisonous roots that, if eaten, cause convulsions, overproduction of saliva, hyperventilation and profuse perspiration, often with a fatal outcome. The fresh root is used to prepare the homeopathic remedy, which is used as a treatment for injuries and disorders of the central nervous system. Hence it is used to treat spasms, twitchings and muscular jerking, especially when the head and neck are thrown backwards, as may occur in epilepsy, following a head injury, meningitis and eclampsia of pregnancy. The patient may be confused, delirious, agitated and moaning unconsciously. The pupils of the eyes may be dilated. Symptoms are worse for sudden movement, cold and with touch. They improve with warmth and the elimination of abdominal wind. A person who benefits from this remedy may crave unsuitable substances as food.

Cinnamomum

Cinnamon; *Cinnamomum zeylanicum*

There are several varieties of cinnamon but the

Cinnamomum zeylanicum tree is a native species of Sri Lanka and is also grown in several other eastern countries and the West Indies. The tree grows to about 30 feet in height, producing white flowers and, later, blue-coloured berries. The part used is the bark of the shoots, which is dried and rolled into thin brown quills. There is a characteristic pleasant, aromatic smell, and powdered cinnamon is widely used as a spice in food. In homeopathy, the remedy is used to treat bleeding such as nosebleeds and also vomiting, nausea and diarrhoea. Some of the symptoms may be caused by stress or hysteria.

Clematis erecta

Upright virgin's bower

This poisonous perennial plant is a native of many European countries, growing to about three feet in height and having reddish-green leaves and white flowers. The leaves and flowers are acrid and irritant when crushed, producing inflammation and blistering. In homeopathy, the remedy is used mainly in the treatment of gonorrhoea, including blockage of the urethra and a slow flow of urine because of inflammation or scarring. It may be used to treat other inflammations of the genital and urinary tract, eye disorders and neuralgia.

Cocculus

Indian cockle

This remedy, prepared from the body of the whole animal, is used to treat symptoms of nausea, sickness, giddiness and vertigo. Often there is accompanying depression, and, in women, symptoms are worse at the time of the period, which tends to be painful and may be early. A person suitable for this remedy is frequently talkative and hates wearing constricting clothing.

Coffea arabica

Coffea; coffee

The coffee tree is a native of Arabia but has been cultivated for many years in other tropical countries. In addition to having been widely used for many centuries as a drink, coffee has been valued medically for its stimulant, analgesic and diuretic properties. The plant has dark green, shiny, evergreen leaves and produces attractive white flowers. Later, berries are formed, which are bright orange-red when ripe, containing the seeds or coffee beans. The beans are roasted for use as a drink, but the unroasted beans are used to prepare the Coffea remedy. Coffea is used to treat insomnia when the brain is over-active and the person cannot relax enough to fall asleep. It is a useful remedy for any form of over-excitability and also severe pain such as toothache and painful labour. The person is very sensitive to noise, touch, disturbance or odours of any kind, and symptoms are made worse by cold winds. They improve with warmth and resting in quiet, calm, peaceful surroundings.

Colchicum autumnale

Colchicum; naked ladies, meadow saffron

This attractive flower grows from a bulbous structure called a corm, which is an underground swollen stem. The pretty light purple flowers appear in September and October (hence 'autumnale') and it grows on limestone soils throughout Europe, parts of Asia, North America and Canada. The plant has been well known since ancient times for its medicinal properties, being especially valued by Greek physicians for the treatment of painful rheumatic and gouty joints. It was known as the 'soul of joints'. It is poisonous, irritant and emetic in larger doses, having an effect on the digestive organs and kidneys. The fresh bulb is used to prepare the homeopathic remedy, which is used to treat severe painful gout, especially of the big toe, and digestive upset including nausea, sickness, diarrhoea and abdominal pains that are relieved if the body is bent forwards. Symptoms are made worse by cold, damp weather, especially in the autumn, and by exercise or being touched. They improve with warmth, and resting in quiet surroundings.

Conium maculatum

Conium; hemlock, spotted hemlock, poison hemlock, poison parsley, beaver poison, spotted corobane, musquash root

This highly poisonous plant grows widely throughout Europe, parts of Asia, Canada, the United States of America and South America. It has been well known and used for centuries and is described in the writings of the ancient Greeks and Romans, including Pliny and Dioscorides. It was used as a means of execution of criminals, and Socrates was forced to drink the fatal poison of hemlock. Roman physicians used hemlock to treat a number of different disorders, including tumours and swellings of the joints and skin, cancer of the breast, liver diseases and as a sedative for spasms and dysfunction of nerves and muscles. Since it induces paralysis, it was used to combat pain and also to control inappropriate sexual feelings. Hemlock is a tall plant that may reach a height of four feet, producing large, indented green leaves and heads of white flowers. The stalks are streaked with purply-red, which, one old legend suggests, is a reminder of the mark on the forehead of Cain, the first murderer. Juice obtained from the leaves and stems of hemlock is used to prepare the homeopathic remedy, which is used for enlarged and hardened glands, including the prostate gland, cancerous tumours and nodules, particularly of the breast, painful breasts before and during periods or because of pregnancy. The remedy is also used for nerve and muscle paralysis, especially that which gradually creeps up the legs and in which there may additionally be a dislike of strong light. It is used to treat premature ejaculation and dizziness that increases when the person lies down or moves the head. In general, the symptoms are made worse by suppression of sexual needs or an excess of sexual activity. Watching a moving object and drinking alcohol also make the symptoms worse. They improve with continued pressure applied to the painful part, sustained gentle exercise and if there is abdominal flatulence. People who benefit from Conium tend to have rather fixed and narrow ideas and a lack of interest in the wider world, which causes depression and a feeling of boredom and apathy. These feelings may be caused either by an over-indulgence in, or too little, sexual activity. Conium people do not cope well if forced to be celibate.

Crocus sativus

Crocus, saffron crocus, saffron

Crocus sativus is a native of the western parts of Asia but has long been cultivated throughout Europe, especially in Spain. The three long, deep orange-red stigmas within the crocus flower are the source of saffron, which has been used medicinally since ancient times. Saffron is mentioned in the Old Testament Song of Solomon (4 :14) and was described by Hippocrates as having aphrodisiac and purgative qualities. It was used to treat uterine bleeding disorders and prolonged and painful childbirth as well as diseases of the liver. Throughout history it has been used to treat a wide variety of physical and mental disorders. In homeopathy the remedy is used to treat disorders of menstruation and nosebleeds and also emotional symptoms of weepiness, depression and mood swings. The symptoms are made worse by warm, stuffy surroundings and listening to music. They improve out in the fresh open air and after eating breakfast.

Crotalus homolus

Crotalus hor.; venom of the rattlesnake

The rattlesnake is familiar to people throughout the world, far beyond its normal habitat in the dry, semi-desert regions of the United States, Canada, Mexico and South America. Its most noteworthy characteristic is the rattling tail, which the snake uses as a warning when it is agitated or about to strike, and the animal has been widely described and depicted in books, films and nature programmes. The snake produces a potent venom that it uses to paralyse its prey, and this was investigated and proved in 1837 by Dr Constantine Hering, an outstanding American homeopathic doctor. In modern homeopathy the remedy is used to treat serious illnesses such as strokes affecting the right side of the body, symptoms of liver failure (including jaundice and oedema), cancer and heart disease. The remedy helps to arrest bleeding from a natural orifice of the body and is used to treat septicaemia, shock and collapse. The symptoms are worse for lying on the left side and for wearing constricting, tight clothing. Humid, warm, moist weather aggravates the symptoms but they are better out in the fresh, clean, dry air.

Croton tiglium

Croton oil seeds

This small, shrubby bush is a native species of the coastal regions of India and Asia, and produces fruits that each contain a single seed rich in oil. Croton oil is obtained by compressing the ripe seeds, and in its neat form is highly purgative if taken internally, producing colicky abdominal pains, diarrhoea and vomiting. It may prove fatal if more than one small dose is taken. Applied externally, it produces irritation and blistering of the skin. In herbal medicine it is used to treat severe constipation, often combined with castor oil, and also as a counterirritant in some rheumatic, bronchitic and other disorders. In homeopathy, the remedy is used to treat severe digestive symptoms of colic-type abdominal pains, copious watery diarrhoea and vomiting. Also, it is used for severe skin inflammations in which there is redness, heat and blistering.

Cyclamen europaeum

Cyclamen; sowbread

There are several species of cyclamen, many of which are native to the warmer countries of southern Europe and northern Africa. The plant has a large, swollen, brown root and derives its common name from the fact that these tubers were a source of food for wild pigs. Cyclamen was used by the physicians of ancient Greece and Rome and also Arabia. It was used to treat disorders of the liver and spleen, including jaundice and hepatitis, and to regulate periods in women. The plant produces very pretty pink flowers, each borne on a single firm, fleshy stalk, and varieties of cyclamen are very popular as house plants. The fresh root is extremely acrid and acts as a purgative, and is used for this purpose in herbal medicine. In homeopathy the sap from the fresh root is used to prepare the remedy, which is used for an irregular menstrual cycle in women. It is also helpful in the treatment of searing, hot pains in the muscles or skin and severe migraine-like headaches with disturbance of vision. People who benefit from this remedy may crave bizarre and inappropriate things to eat. They tend to have a melancholy disposition, often feeling sad and depressed or beset by guilt or remorse. Symptoms are made better by exercise and moving around and with crying. They improve in the fresh open air.

Datura stramonium

Stramonium; thorn apple, devil's apple, stinkweed, devil's trumpet, Jamestown weed, Jimson weed

There are a number of species of *Datura* distributed throughout many countries of the world, and all are poisonous with highly narcotic effects. *Datura stramonium* is found in Europe, North America and Asia, often growing as a weed on waste ground. It is a large, bushy plant, usually about three or four feet in height and producing large white flowers. Later, pebble-sized capsules protected by thorns are produced that open when ripe to reveal black or very dark brown seeds. The flowers have a pleasant scent, but the rest of the plant, especially the leaves, give off an unpleasant, rank smell that is repellent to grazing animals. The plant has been used in herbal medicine for many hundreds of years. Inhalation of the smoke from the burning plant was used as a cure for attacks of asthma, and sometimes a type of cigarette was made from the leaves for this purpose. Preparations of the plant were used externally to relieve painful rheumatism, neuralgic conditions such as sciatica, haemorrhoids, abscesses and boils, and other inflammations. It has also been used for sedation and was eaten by soldiers in medieval Europe before going into battle to calm their fears. Juice extracted from the green parts of the plant before it comes into flower are used to prepare the homeopathic remedy. It is used to treat nervous system disorders and is a useful remedy for children. Symptoms include muscular jerking, spasms and twitches, convulsions because of epilepsy, high fever in children or meningitis and strokes. Also, for physical symptoms suffered by a person who has sustained a severe shock or fright, night terrors in children, states of great anxiety and mental agitation. A child may be terrified of the dark and the imagined creatures of the night. An adult may have a fear of water or is unreasonably afraid that he or she may suffer violence. The person often has a craving for drinks of an acidic nature and has an excessive thirst. Symptoms are worse if the person is left alone and following sleep. Also, when the person tries to swallow liquids or food and if the weather is overcast and cloudy. The symptoms improve if the person has the reassurance and company of other people, particularly if the surroundings are light, airy and warm.

Delphinium staphysagria

Staphysagria; stavesacre, staphisagris, planted larkspur, lousewort

This plant has a long history of medicinal use going back to the civilizations of ancient Greece and Rome, being described by both Dioscorides and Pliny. It was used externally to destroy parasites such as lice and to treat insect bites and stings, and has continued to be employed for this purpose throughout history. It is highly poisonous and even in small doses causes vomiting and diarrhoea, acting as a purgative. Staphysagria is a large, annual plant with hairy stems and leaves, which grows to a height of about four feet and is a native of southern European and Asian countries. It produces spikes of light blue/purple flowers and, later, seed pods containing dark-coloured seeds. The seeds are the part used in both herbal medicine and homeopathy. The homeopathic remedy is used to treat neuralgic pains, toothache, pain from the incision of an operation, pressure headache, inflammation and infection of the eyes or eyelids, such as styes and blepharitis, cystitis and painful sexual intercourse in women. It may also be used for painful teething in young children and for disorders of the prostate gland in men. Usually, the person who benefits has suppressed anger or resentment and is inclined to be irritable. Symptoms are made worse for suppression of feelings, following a sleep in the afternoon and after eating breakfast. They improve with warmth and by giving voice to the emotions. People suitable for staphysagria appear equable and mild on the outside but internally seethe with suppressed emotions, especially anger. They are inclined to harbour resentment for supposed slights or insults and are somewhat driven, workaholic people. They often have a high libido and suppress their emotions because they are afraid of losing self-control, especially in front of other people. Body secretions may smell unpleasant, and they have a desire for alcoholic drinks and sweetened foods.

Digitalis purpurea

Digitalis; foxglove, fairy thimbles, fairy's gloves, witch's gloves, folk's glove

The striking and attractive foxglove, with its deep pink-purple, long, bell-shaped flowers, is a familiar plant in Britain and other European countries. One of its oldest name, folk's glove, associates it with the 'good folk', or fairies, who were believed to inhabit the woods and groves where the plant commonly grows. The name foxglove is derived from Anglo-Saxon, but the plant was given its Latin adjective of *Digitalis* in the mid-16th century, derived from *digitabulum*, meaning 'thimble'. The plant was used medicinally in ancient times as a cure for wounds and bruising. It was not until 1785, however, that its value in the treatment of dropsy (oedema, or fluid retention, which may accompany heart disease) was discovered by a Dr William Withering. Its main use, both in modern orthodox medicine and homeopathy, is as a major remedy for heart disorders. Liquid extracted from the new fresh green leaves collected in the spring is used to prepare the homeopathic remedy. It is used as a treatment for a slow, faint or irregular heartbeat such as may accompany heart failure and other heart and circulatory disorders. The person often experiences a sinking sensation in the pit of the stomach such as occurs with fear and may feel that the heart is about to cease to beat altogether. There may be additional problems, particularly with the liver or kidneys. The symptoms are made worse by listening to music, eating a meal and sitting in an upright position. They improve out in the fresh open air and by not eating. The person who benefits from this remedy may feel nauseated at the sight of food.

Dioscorea villosa

Dioscorea; wild yam, rheumatism root, colic root, wild yamwurzel

This perennial plant is a native species of Canada and the United States, although there are many other varieties inhabiting most tropical countries. It has a twining habit with a long, twisted, branched root that is the part used to prepare the homeopathic remedy. Preparations of the root act upon the smooth muscle of the digestive tract, having antispasmodic properties. Hence the remedy is used to treat spasmodic colicky pains, bilious colic, morning sickness during pregnancy, abdominal wind and diarrhoea. Other types of spasmodic pain, such as neuralgia, may benefit from this remedy, and symptoms are relieved by gentle exercise and movement.

Duboisia myoporoides

Duboisia; corkwood elm, corkwood tree

This large shrub or small tree is a native species of Australia, producing large, white flowers and green leaves that are gathered when the plant is flowering to prepare the homeopathic remedy. The preparation made from the leaves acts on the central nervous system, having an hypnotic and sedative effect. Applied to the eye it is a mydriatic, causing dilation of the pupil. In homeopathy, the remedy is used for eye disorders, particularly if there are one or more floating red spots (debris) causing disturbance of vision. Also, for painful, irritated and inflamed eyes such as may be caused by conjunctivitis. It may be used for symptoms of vertigo or where there are symptoms of mental confusion.

Dryopteris filix-mas

Male shield fern

A common type of fern found in the United Kingdom, Europe and many other countries with a temperate climate. The plant has a stocky, short rhizome or underground stem just beneath the surface of the soil, with a tangle of roots protruding from its under surface. This part is collected and dried and used to prepare remedies both in herbal and homeopathic medicine. The root contains a liquid oleoresin and has been known since ancient times for its anthelmintic properties (anti-worm), being particularly useful for the expulsion of a tapeworm. One method, using the root of the fern, is described by Dioscorides, and the remedy continues to be used for this purpose today. If a tapeworm is present there may be little in the way of symptoms but abdominal cramps, slight bleeding and itching. One dose is usually sufficient to expel the parasite, and preparations have also been used in veterinary medicine.

Elaps corallinus

Corallinus; coral snake

The attractive coral snake is a native animal of North and South America, especially Brazil and Canada. The snake has broad red and narrower blue bands of colour down the length of its body that are separated from one another by thin strips of white. The homeopathic remedy is prepared from fresh snake venom and is used as a treatment for troublesome bleeding and strokes. The bleeding disorders that may benefit from Elaps include nosebleeds, heavy menstruation (menorrhagia), piles and strokes affecting the right side of the body. The person may have a feeling of being chilled inside and desire cold drinks. However, cold foods and drinks, humid weather before a thunderstorm and getting too hot in bed make the symptoms worse. Also, they are worse if the person lies on his or her front or walks around. Symptoms are generally better during the night and for staying still. People who benefit from Elaps are usually afraid of snakes and fear being left on their own and do not like the rain. They are frightened of death and the possibility of having a stroke.

Equisetum hiemale, Equisetum arvense

Equisetum; horsetail, scouring rush, pewterwort, bottlebrush, shave-grass, paddock-pipes

The horsetails are a very ancient group of plants descended from species that grew during the Carboniferous geological period. Several species are found in the British Isles. *Equisetum arvense* is the most common of these and is also distributed in many other countries of the world. *Equisetum hiemale* is found in China and other eastern countries. Horsetails produce two kinds of stems, fertile and barren, which are jointed and hollow. There are no leaves but long green spikes at the joints with jagged edges. The fruiting or fertile stem, which is produced early in the season before the barren stems appear, has a cone-like structure at the end containing numerous spores. The stems of horsetails are strengthened with silica, and the plants were formerly used for scouring and cleaning purposes (hence the names pewterwort, scouring brush, bottlebrush, etc). There is a long history of medicinal use going back to ancient times, and the plant is described by Dioscorides as being good for the healing of wounds. While the plant continued to be used for wounds and ulcers, it was also believed to be helpful in the healing of ruptures and for bowel and kidney complaints. In modern herbal medicine, it is used for kidney disorders and fluid retention (oedema) as it has diuretic as well as astringent properties. The fresh parts of the plant are used to prepare the homeopathic remedy, which is used to treat an irritable bladder. The symptoms resemble those of cystitis but without the presence of infection. The bladder feels constantly full with an aching and dragging sensation. There is a continual feeling of the need to pass urine, which is usually released only in small amounts with pain at the end of urination. There may be kidney pain and slight incontinence. Equisetum is a useful remedy for children who wet the bed when suffering from disturbed sleep because of nightmares. The symptoms are worse if pressure is applied to the painful part and with touch, exercise or movement. They improve if the person remains still and lies on the back.

Euonymus atropurpurea

Euonymus; burning bush, wahoo, Indian arrowroot

This shrub is a native species of the United States and grows to a height of about six feet. It produces attractive deep purple flowers and dark green leaves that are edged with a purple tinge. The bark of the roots and stems is used and, in small doses, the preparation has a stimulant effect on the digestive system. However, in large doses it has an irritant and purgative effect. In herbal medicine, it is valued as a liver stimulant promoting the flow of bile juice. The homeopathic remedy is used for digestive complaints with bloatedness and abdominal pain and swelling of the feet and ankles because of retention of fluid (oedema). There may be stomach irritation (gastritis) with diarrhoea or blood in the stools. The remedy is also used for mental symptoms of irritability or confusion.

Euonymus europea

Spindle tree, prickwood, skewerwood, fusanum, fusoria

The spindle tree grows in woods and hedges in the British Isles and other European countries. It produces clusters of white flowers tinged with green in early summer and, later, bright red fruits containing orange seeds. The leaves, fruits and bark are all harmful and are not touched by grazing animals. The fruits cause severe sickness and diarrhoea if eaten, and the seeds are used to prepare the homeopathic remedy. It is used to treat digestive disorders with severe abdominal pains and copious diarrhoea. Also, for symptoms of angina, including constricting chest pains and breathlessness. Symptoms may occur mainly on the left side.

Eupatorium perfoliatum

Eupator; boneset, thoroughwort, agueweed, feverwort

This perennial plant is a native species of North America,

being common on damp ground in low-lying situations. It is a very important plant in herbal medicine and has always been valued for its medicinal uses, firstly by the Indian native peoples and later by European and African settlers. It has a thick hairy stem and abundant white flowers throughout the summer months. Preparations made from the plant act as a tonic or stimulant of the digestive system in small doses. However, in large doses it causes sickness and diarrhoea, having a purgative effect. It is also valued for its fever-reducing qualities and, in addition, is diaphoretic, promoting perspiration. The whole green plant and flowers are used to prepare the homeopathic remedy, which is given for feverish conditions such as colds and influenza. Accompanying symptoms include restlessness, severe aches and pains in the bones, hot, dry skin and little perspiration. The person craves ice-cold drinks and foods, such as ice cream, and may have a painful, dry cough. Symptoms are worse for exercise and movement and in the early morning between 7 a.m. and 9 a.m. Also, they are worse outside in fresh clean air. They are better inside and for talking to other people and for vomiting bile.

Ferrum metallicum

Ferrum met.; iron

Iron is a very important mineral in the body, being a part of the haemoglobin molecule. Haemoglobin is the iron-containing pigment in red blood cells that combines with oxygen in the lungs from where it is transported and supplied to all cells and tissues. If there is a deficiency of iron in the blood, which can arise for a number of different reasons, the result is anaemia. The person becomes pale, tired and breathless, especially with any form of exertion, and body systems cannot function properly. Iron is widely used in conventional medicine as well as homeopathy. The source is iron ore, and haematite, a red-coloured bulbous deposit found in association with various rocks, particularly in North America, Canada and Venezuela, is especially rich in this mineral. The homeopathic remedy is used for circulatory disorders and anaemia. The person is frequently tired and listless, looks pale and feels chilled and may have cold hands and feet, but at the same time is often restless. The person soon becomes exhausted and may be breathless with physical exertion. The tiredness may cause irritability, depression and changes of mood. People suitable for Ferrum met. are frequently well built and appear robust but suffer from the symptoms described above. They dislike food rich in fat or cholesterol but enjoy pickled and sour foods. They may be allergic to eggs but like tomatoes.

Fluoricum acidum

Fluor. ac.; hydrofluoric acid

Hydrofluoric acid has several industrial uses, particularly

in the manufacture of metals and glassware, being used for cleaning and etching. It is obtained by a distillation process involving sulphuric acid and calcium fluoride with the production of hydrogen fluoride gas. When this gas is passed through water it dissolves to give hydrofluoric acid, which contains fluorine. Fluorine is an important constituent of teeth and bones and is a strengthening substance. The homeopathic remedy is used to treat disorders of connective tissue, bones and teeth. Varicose veins and ulcers, bone pain and tumours and decaying, softened teeth may benefit from Fluor ac. People suitable for this remedy are frequently rather selfish and self-centred and not inclined to commit themselves to others. They are worldly and materialistic and tend to judge success in life in financial terms. Fluor. ac. people lack spiritual and emotional understanding and may have a high sex drive. They manage with little sleep and are very active, seldom feeling cold or tired.

Formica rufa

Red ant

The homeopathic remedy is obtained from the body of the crushed red ant. It is suitable for conditions producing symptoms of hot, burning, stabbing pains such as may affect joints, as in arthritic, rheumatic and gouty disorders. It is also used for severe headaches and numbness affecting the face. There may be an inability to concentrate, vagueness or slight forgetfulness.

Fragaria vesca

Wild strawberry, wood strawberry

This plant is a native species of most European countries, including Britain. It is a low, creeping plant with a tangle of stalks and leaves, and produces white flowers followed by small red berries that are covered with tiny seeds. The flavour of the fruit is delicious and fragrant and has long been valued as food. The fruit, and especially the leaves, have been used for hundreds of years for medicinal purposes, the plant having diuretic, astringent and laxative properties. Preparations made from the plant were used to treat kidney stones and urinary complaints, wounds, gout, tooth decay and diarrhoea. The cut strawberries rubbed on the skin help to relieve sunburn and other skin complaints and remove stains when applied to the teeth. The homeopathic remedy is used to alleviate an allergic reaction to strawberries, especially when this causes a skin rash and itching. It is also used for stones in the kidneys or gall bladder, a build-up of tartar on the teeth and chilblains or sunburn.

Fraxinus americana

American white ash

Ash trees of the genus *Fraxinus* have been used for medicinal purposes in many different countries. Various parts of the plant have been used, especially the bark, leaves, fruit and 'keys'. The bark of the American white ash, which grows in the United States, is used to prepare a homeopathic remedy. It has astringent and tonic properties and is used in homeopathy to treat a prolapsed uterus with dragging lower abdominal pain and also for fibroids.

Gentiana cruciata

Cross-leaved gentian

There are many species of gentian found in most countries throughout the world. In all varieties the plant, and especially the root, is extremely bitter and is used as a tonic medicine. The cross-leaved gentian, with leaves growing in the shape of a cross, has been used in herbal medicine as a treatment for hydrophobia (rabies). In homeopathy, the root is used to prepare the remedy, which is given for a sore throat or hoarseness, gastritis and infections of the stomach, colicky pains, nausea, sickness and diarrhoea and hernia.

Gentiana lutea

Yellow gentian

The yellow gentian is a native species of the mountainous, alpine and sub-alpine pastures of Europe although it does not occur naturally in the British Isles. It has a long root exceeding one foot in length, and the stalk grows to a height of three or four feet. The leaves are a yellow-green colour, and the plant produces attractive, large, deep orange-yellow flowers. The root is collected and dried to make medicinal preparations and has long been valued for its bitter, tonic properties. In homeopathy, it is used as a remedy for digestive problems and gastritis with symptoms of griping abdominal pains, nausea, vomiting and diarrhoea, heartburn and bloatedness.

Glonoinum

Glonoin; nitroglycerine, glyceryl trinitrate

This substance, which occurs as a clear, poisonous, oily liquid, is derived from a chemical process and was discovered in the mid-1800s by an Italian chemist. It is prepared by mixing together certain proportions of sulphuric acid and nitric acid and then adding glycerine. The addition of diatomaceous earth or kiesel-guhr (a natural deposit of sediment composed of the silica skeletons of minute marine creatures called diatoms) to nitroglycerine, produces dynamite. This extremely dangerous explosive was first formulated by the eminent Swedish scientist, Alfred Nobel, in 1867. Nitroglycerine acts very strongly on the heart and blood circulation and is used in conventional medicine as a remedy for the symptoms of angina. In homeopathy the remedy is also used for symptoms affecting the blood circulation and head caused by a sudden, increased rush of blood. Symptoms include a feeling of congestion in the head with a pounding, severe headache, hot flushes and sweats. The person may try to relieve the pain by holding and pressing the head between the hands. Also, it is used in the treatment of heat exhaustion and the early symptoms of heatstroke. The symptoms are made worse by any kind of movement, especially turning the head, and by heat. They are relieved by cold and being out in cool, fresh air.

Helleborus niger

Christmas rose, Christ herb, melampode, black hellebore

The Christmas rose is a highly poisonous plant that is found naturally in the mountainous regions of southern, central and eastern Europe. It is known as a garden plant in the British Isles and derives its name of black hellebore from the colour of the root. It flowers in the depths of winter, from which comes its association with Christmas and Christ. The plant has large, serrated, dark-green leaves and white flowers tinged with pink, but it is the dark-coloured rhizome and root that are used to prepare the herbal and homeopathic remedies. The plant has been known since ancient times and is described in the writings of Pliny. It was used as a cure for various ailments in cattle and other domestic animals, and has strong purgative and narcotic effects. It also has a powerful effect on the kidneys, heart and uterus. In homeopathy, it is used in the treatment of severe headaches with stabbing pain that may be associated with a former head injury. There may be symptoms of mental confusion, mood changes or even convulsions or epilepsy. Slight movements make the symptoms worse, as do cold draughts of air.

Hydrastis canadensis

Hydrastis; golden seal, yellow puccoon, orange root, Indian dye, Indian paint, eye balm, eye root, ground raspberry

This plant is a native species of Canada and the eastern United States, and has a long history of medicinal use, firstly by the Indian peoples, particularly the Cherokees, and later by Europeans. It is a small, perennial plant growing to a height of about six to twelve inches and producing a greenish white flower and later an inedible fruit resembling a raspberry. There is a knotty, yellow-brown tangled root system from which a dye was extracted and used by the Indians to colour their clothes and skin. The fresh root or rhizome (underground stem) is the part used medicinally. It was used by the Indian peoples to treat digestive disorders, liver complaints, eye irritations, ulcers, cancer, heart conditions and fevers. It has a particular effect on mucous membranes, making it useful in the treatment of catarrh, and has tonic, cleansing and astringent properties. The homeopathic remedy was investigated and proved by the American homeopath Dr Hale in 1875, although the plant had been known in Europe since the mid-18th century. In homeopathy the remedy is used to treat catarrhal complaints such as may occur with infections of the nose and throat and chest. Typically, a thick, yellow catarrh is produced, and there may be a sore throat and other pains. It is also used for digestive disorders in which there may be persistent constipation, nausea and vomiting and loss of appetite and weight. It is particularly useful as a tonic for people who have lost weight because of a long, debilitating illness. The symptoms are worse in the evening and night and out in cold air. They are relieved by rest, quiet and warm surroundings.

Hyoscyamus niger

Hyoscyamus; henbane, henbell, hogbean

Henbane grows widely throughout Europe and western Asia, and has been introduced and become naturalised in North America, Canada and parts of South America, such as Brazil. It is believed that it may have been brought to Britain and other European countries by the Romans, and it is described by both Dioscorides and Pliny. The plant is poisonous, narcotic and sedative, and was used by ancient physicians to induce sleep and relieve pain. Henbane has a varied habit, occurring as both annual and biennial forms. Both are used medicinally, although the biennial form is generally considered to be more useful. The preparations are narcotic, hypnotic and antispasmodic in effect, and are used in conventional medicine to treat spasms of the digestive tract. Juice extracted from the fresh whole flowering plant is used to prepare the homeopathic remedy, which is used for mental and emotional problems.

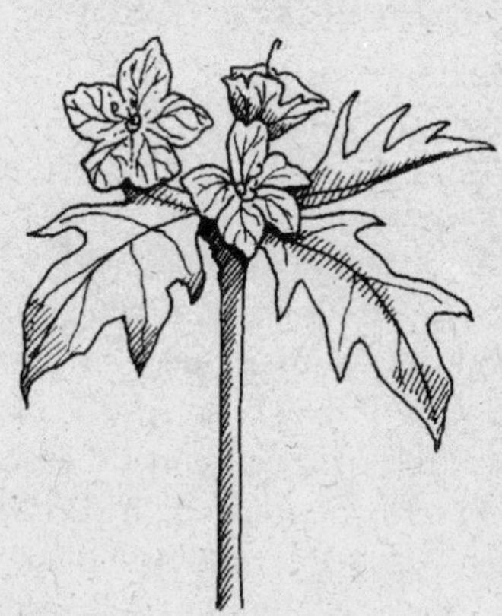

Symptoms include paranoia and suspicion of others, unreasonable behaviour and jealousy, delusions, aggressive outbursts and the use of foul and sexually suggestive language. Henbane is also used to relieve the physical symptoms of muscular spasms and cramp-like intermittent pains that may accompany epilepsy, disorders of the digestive system and bladder. Symptoms are made worse by lying down and being touched, with being covered up and for any emotional upheaval. They are relieved if the person sits in an upright position.

Iberis amara

Bitter candytuft

This small, flowering annual plant grows throughout Europe and is a familiar garden flower. It grows to a height of about six inches and produces white or pink flowers in the summer months. All parts of the plant are used in herbal medicine, but the seeds alone are gathered and prepared to make a tincture used in homeopathy. The remedy was investigated and proved by the American homeopath Dr Edwin Hale, and it is used to treat heart disorders. It may be given for angina, palpitations, oedema, breathlessness and chest pains. It is also a treatment for bronchitis and asthma and sickness and vertigo.

Iodum

Iodine

Iodine is a nonmetallic element that is an essential substance for the normal functioning of metabolic processes within the body. It is mainly concentrated in the thyroid gland and is a major component of thyroid hormones, which themselves regulate many body processes. A deficiency of iodine causes a gain in weight, swelling of the face and neck, a dry skin and mental apathy. The person feels excessively tired, and the hair starts to fall out. This deficiency is not usually seen in western countries because iodine is added to table salt. Iodine is found naturally in seaweed and deposits of saltpetre (an evaporate mineral found in dry, desert-like conditions, particularly in Chile). Tincture of iodine is used in homeopathy as a remedy for hyperthyroidism (an overactive thyroid gland). The symptoms include weakness and wasting, noticed especially in the limbs, pain and bulging of the eyes, excessive hunger, restlessness, nervousness, sweating, breathlessness, intolerance of heat and rapid heart beat. It is also used for severe, hacking coughs, shortness of breath, laryngitis and throat disorders and pain in the bones. People who benefit from this remedy like to be busy and may be talkative and excitable. However, they may also be forgetful so that their activities may be inefficient and disorganised. Symptoms are made worse by heat in any form and are relieved by cool, fresh air. They also improve for movement and exercise and after meals.

Iris versicolor

The blue flag, water flag, poison flag, liver lily, flag lily, snake lily, dagger flower, dragon flower

This attractive but poisonous flowering plant is a native species of North America and Canada, growing in damp, low-lying conditions. It is a popular garden plant in the British Isles, growing to a height of about two or three feet and producing deep blue-purple flowers. Preparations made from the rhizome have a diuretic and stimulant effect and cause sickness and diarrhoea. They are mainly used for liver and digestive complaints. The fresh rhizome or underground stem is used to prepare the homeopathic remedy, which is used for indigestion, vomiting and nausea, diarrhoea, colicky pains and also for migraine where the headache is on the right side.

Kali bromatum

Kali brom.; potassium bromide

This white, crystalline substance, which is obtained from a chemical process, is used in the photographic industry and has also been given as a remedy in conventional medicine. It was given to men to reduce an excessive libido and particularly to male prisoners. It was also given for some other psychiatric disorders and as a treatment for epilepsy. The homeopathic remedy is given as a treatment for severe acne and skin disorders, excessive menstrual bleeding especially during the menopause, impotence, epilepsy, nervous exhaustion and depression. People suitable for Kali brom. tend to be restless and anxious and have a need to be busy. During their teenage years they may require a lot of reassurance and tend to feel guilty about their emerging sexuality. They may have strong religious beliefs and feel that sexual needs are immoral, and this causes mental stress and conflict. They are prone to acne, especially at puberty and during times of hormonal change. In women, symptoms are worse during menstruation. All symptoms improve if the person is fully occupied.

Kali sulphuricum

Potassium sulphate

Potassium sulphate is another of the SCHUSSLER TISSUE SALTS (*see* Glossary), which is used in homeopathy for catarrhal conditions in which there is a thick white or yellow discharge. This may occur in bronchitis and other infections of the nose and throat. Also, it is used to treat infected skin conditions, such as erysipelas and eczema, in which there is a pus-like discharge. It may be used as a remedy for such infectious illnesses as measles and scarlet fever, which affect the skin, and also for rheumatism. Symptoms are made worse by hot surroundings and heat in any form and are relieved by coldness and fresh air.

Kalium carbonicum

Kali carb; potassium carbonate

Potassium carbonate occurs naturally in all plants, and is obtained from the ash of burnt wood or other vegetation, or by a chemical process. Potassium carbonate was used by the ancient Egyptian civilisation in the manufacture of glassware. The remedy is used for complaints affecting the mucous membranes of the upper respiratory system and digestive organs. It is used for coughs and bronchitis with stitch-like pains, menopausal and menstrual problems, pains in the back and head. The person feels cold and fluid is retained (oedema), causing swelling of the face, especially the upper eyelids. The person feels chilled and may be likely to catch colds or influenza. Symptoms are worse for physical exertion, bending the body forwards and for cool conditions. They are worse in the very early morning between 2 and 3 a.m. Symptoms improve in warm, dry conditions and weather. People who are suitable for all the Kalium remedies have a strict sense of duty and firm ideas about right and wrong. They are possessive and may be jealous and difficult to live with. They cope badly with any kind of emotional trauma and may feel as though they have been kicked in the abdomen if they receive upsetting news.

Kalium muriaticum

Kali mur.; potassium chloride

This white or colourless crystalline substance is found naturally as the mineral sylvite, which occurs in beds of evaporite deposits. It is much used as a fertiliser, and in homeopathy is one of the Schussler tissue salts (*see* Glossary). A deficiency of potassium chloride affects blood-clotting capability. The Kali mur. remedy is used to treat inflammations and infections of the mucous membranes. Typically, there is a thick, mucus discharge, and this may occur with middle ear and throat infections, glue ear in children and tonsillitis. The throat may be very sore and swallowing painful and difficult, and the person may have a fever and swollen glands. Symptoms are worse in cold, damp weather and in cold fresh air. Also, they feel worse for eating fatty foods and, in women, during a period. Symptoms are better for sipping ice-cold drinks and for gently rubbing the painful part.

Kalmia latifolia

American laurel, broad-leaved laurel, sheep laurel, calico bush, lambkill, kalmia

An attractive but poisonous evergreen shrub that is a native species of some states of the United States of America. It grows to a height of anything up to twenty feet and produces an abundance of pink flowers. The leaves are the part of the plant used medicinally, and they have narcotic and astringent properties and also sedative effects on the heart. The plant was known to the native Indian people and has been used in the treatment of skin diseases, fevers, syphilis, neuralgia, blood disorders, haemorrhages, diarrhoea and dysentery. The homeopathic remedy is made from the fresh leaves of the plant and is used to treat symptoms occurring on the right side of the body, such as facial and other neuralgia, shingles, rheumatic pains, numbness and paralysis, and heart problems such as angina. Symptoms are made worse by cold in any form, touch or pressure, and are relieved by warmth.

Kreosotum

Creosote in spirits

This remedy is used for infected conditions in which there is pus or other discharge that often has an offensive smell. Hence it is used for skin eruptions such as boils, gum disease and tooth decay with bad breath, and infections of the womb, bladder, pelvic organs and prostate gland. The person may suffer from general weakness and debility with nausea, vomiting, diarrhoea and colicky pains. Symptoms may occur mainly on the left side.

Lac caninum

Lac. can.; milk from a female dog, bitch's milk

This is one of the oldest known remedies, being described

by a physician of ancient Greece, Sextus, who used it for treating ear infections and sensitivity to light. Pliny referred to its usefulness in treating female reproductive disorders, and this is one of its uses in homeopathy. The homeopathic remedy is used in the treatment of erosion of the cervix, in which cells that line the neck of the womb are worn away. It is also used for sore breasts during breast-feeding or before menstruation. Another major use is in the treatment of severe sore throats, as in tonsillitis, and for diphtheria. The pains or other symptoms often switch from one side of the body to another and may be accompanied by malaise and weakness. The person may feel light-headed, experiencing a floating sensation. People suitable for Lac. can. tend to be highly sensitive, over-imaginative to the point of allowing imagined fears to take over, timid and forgetful. In contrast to this, they are capable on occasion of being unreasonable and aggressive. They have many fears and often experience nightmares, and may have a phobia about snakes. Lac. can. people enjoy spicy salty food and hot drinks. Symptoms are made worse by touch or pressure and improve out in the fresh air.

Lactrodectus mactans

Lactrodectus mac.; female black widow spider

The female black widow is one of the most poisonous of spiders, and its venom can rapidly prove fatal. The venom is injected when the spider bites and produces symptoms of severe, constricting chest pains, sweating, spasm in muscles and blood vessels, fear, collapse and death. The spider is found in a number of countries with a hot climate, particularly in some parts of the United States. The homeopathic remedy is derived from the body of the female spider and is used to treat serious heart complaints including heart attack and angina. It is also used for states of great anxiety and fear with hyperventilation, agitation, breathlessness and collapse. Symptoms are made worse by cold, damp weather and in oppressive conditions before a storm breaks. They are worse at night but improve with reassurance and sitting still and with taking a hot bath.

Lapis albus

Calcium silico-fluoride

This remedy, which is prepared chemically, was investigated and proved by a German homeopathic doctor, Edward von Grauvogl, in the 19th century. It is used to treat hot, stabbing pains in the womb, breasts or stomach and for burning, itchy skin.

Lilium tigrinum

Lilium; tiger lily

This striking flowering plant, which is popular in gardens, is a native species of China and Japan. It produces large, orange flowers that are funnel-shaped with the petals curved back upon themselves. The petals are covered with deep, reddish-coloured spots. The homeopathic remedy, which is made from the whole fresh flowering plant, was investigated and proved in 1869 by the American homeopath Dr Carroll Dunham. It is used for disorders of the female reproductive organs, including a prolapsed uterus with dragging pains, uterine fibroids (benign tumours of the womb) that may affect the bladder, increasing the desire to pass urine, swollen ovaries and ovarian pain, and itching in the genital region. Also, it is given for disorders of the bladder, rectum and veins, and for symptoms of angina. These symptoms include severe constricting chest pain, anxiety and rapid heart beat rate, and a feeling of numbness extending down the right arm. People suitable for this remedy have a very strong sense of right and wrong and set themselves very high standards of behaviour. This may result in conflict between their natural, especially sexual, needs and what they regard as the correct way to behave, leading to feelings of guilt and self-loathing. Their inner turmoil may make them irritable and liable to take offence, especially at remarks that appear to be critical. Lilium people have hot hands and are more comfortable in cool or cold weather. Symptoms are made worse by any form of heat and at night. They improve in cool surroundings and out in the cold fresh air. Symptoms are relieved if the person lies on his or her left side.

Lycopus virginicus

Lycopus; bugleweed, Virginia water, horehound, water bugle, gipsyweed

This attractive plant is a native species of the eastern parts of the United States, growing in damp, low-lying situations in plenty of shade. The plant produces purple-coloured flowers and has smooth, green leaves. It gives off a slightly minty aromatic smell and has astringent, sedative and slightly narcotic properties. It was formerly used to treat bleeding in the lungs, as in tuberculosis, encouraging blood to be coughed up. It has also been used in place of DIGITALIS in the treatment of heart disorders. The whole fresh parts of the plant and flowers are used to prepare the homeopathic remedy, which was first investigated and introduced by the American homeopath, Edwin Moses Hale in the latter part of the 19th century. It is used to treat heart disorders, including abnormalities of the heartbeat and palpitations, aneurysms (balloon-like swellings of artery walls), inflammation of the membranous sac surrounding the heart (pericarditis), raised blood pressure and heart failure. It is also used to treat a disorder of the thyroid gland that produces a protrusion of the eyes. Symptoms are made worse by physical activity and exertion, agitation or excitement and heat in any form. The symptoms are usually worse following sleep but are relieved by pressure on the affected part.

Lyssin

Hydrophobinum

This remedy is prepared from the saliva of a dog that has contracted rabies. It is used for serious disorders of the nervous system, especially convulsions that may be related to epilepsy, severe headaches and pre-eclampsia of pregnancy (a condition marked by retention of fluid and swelling of feet and ankles, high blood pressure and the presence of protein in the urine). If not treated, pre-eclampsia may lead to full eclampsia of pregnancy, which is a life-threatening condition marked by convulsions. The fits intensify if the person is in the presence of running water.

Magnesia carbonica

Mag. carb.; magnesium carbonate

Magnesium carbonate, which is a white, powdery substance, has a variety of industrial uses including the manufacture of bricks, cements, paper, paints and materials for insulation. In pharmaceutical manufacture it is used as a bulking material in some types of powder and tablets. The main source is magnesite, which is formed from altered limestones, dolomites or serpentines and is mined in China, the United States and Austria. The homeopathic remedy was investigated and proved by Hahnemann and is used to treat loss of the sense of taste when there is a thick, whitish coating on the tongue, indigestion and heartburn and digestive complaints with diarrhoea or constipation. The person may have a longing for fruity, acidic drinks and an unpleasant taste in the mouth. This is also a remedy for weakness and failure to thrive in babies where there is a lack of muscle tone. Symptoms are made worse by touch, resting, at night and if conditions are windy. They improve for walking about and being out in fresh, clean air. People suitable for Mag. carb. are often dark-haired and pale-skinned and are prone to exhaustion with pains in the legs and feet. They are very sensitive to cold draughts and being touched and may be on edge and irritable. They are prone to having a sour, unpleasant taste in the mouth and are hypersensitive, being apt to feeling ignored and left out by others. They frequently have an intolerance of milk and sweat, etc, smells sour.

Magnesia phosphorica

Mag. phos.; phosphate of magnesia, magnesium phosphate

This white compound is one of the Schussler tissue salts (*see* GLOSSARY) and is prepared chemically from sodium phosphate and magnesium sulphate. Magnesium occurs naturally in the body and is essential for the correct functioning of nerves and muscles. A deficiency can cause cramping pains and spasms and have deleterious effects on the heart and skeletal muscles. The remedy is used to treat neuralgic pains, writer's cramp, spasms and cramps. The pains are shooting and intermittent and may be brought on by a cold draught. Often, they occur mainly on the right side of the body. Colicky pains that are relieved by doubling over or by bending and by heat and firm pressure, benefit from Mag. phos. People who benefit from this remedy are often thin, sensitive and worried and may be academic, workaholic types. Symptoms are worse for cold air, touch, at night and if the person is tired and debilitated. They improve with any form of heat, pressure and warm surroundings.

Manganum aceticum

Acetate of manganese

This remedy was investigated and proved by Hahnemann in the 19th century. It is useful for the treatment of general debility and weakness with loss of appetite and weight, anaemia and, possibly, ulcers of the skin or bed sores. The skin is a bluish colour, and the body is extremely sensitive to touch. The person has great difficulty in eating enough to maintain body weight.

Medorrhinum

A remedy prepared from gonorrhoeal discharge

Gonorrhoea, the sexually transmitted bacterial disease, has plagued humankind since ancient times, and was first given the name of gonorrhoea by Galen, a physician of the Roman civilisation. The effects of gonorrhoea can be passed from a mother to her baby during birth. Hahnemann believed that gonorrhoea was responsible for inherited traits or weaknesses in subsequent generations, and he called this a 'miasm', in this case the sycotic miasm (sycosis). Two other miasms were identified, 'psora', connected with the blisters and itching of scabies (*see* PSORINUM), and syphilis (*see* SYPHILINUM). Gonorrhoea has always been a feared and devastating illness and was formerly treated with injections of silver nitrate. In conventional medicine it is treated with modern antibiotics.

The homeopathic remedy is used to treat a variety of physical and mental symptoms. It is used to treat inflammation and infection of pelvic organs, menstrual pain and pain in the ovaries. Some other disorders of the mucous membranes, kidneys, nerves and spine, e.g. neuralgia, may benefit from this remedy. It is especially suitable for people who have a family history of gonorrhoea and some forms of heart disease. Emotional disorders may be treated with Medorrhinum, especially mood swings with the person changing from irritability and extreme impatience to passive withdrawal. In the impatient state the person is always in a hurry and is inclined to be selfish and insensitive. In the withdrawn state the person is dreamy and forgetful and very much in touch with, and moved by, the beauty of nature. In both states, the person tends to be forgetful and may feel neglected, lost or deserted. Symptoms are made worse by damp weather, heat in the early morning between 3 and 4 a.m. and after passing urine. Even slight movements make the symptoms worse, but they improve with lying on the front, in the evening and being beside the sea. Symptoms are also better if the person rests on the hands and knees ('all fours').

Mercurius corrosivus

Merc. cor.; mercuric chloride, mercury chloride $HgCl_2$

Mercuric chloride is a highly poisonous corrosive substance, causing burning and destruction of tissue if swallowed. It has antiseptic properties and is used to treat bulbs and tubers to prevent fungal attack. It is also used industrially in the manufacture of plastics. The homeopathic remedy is used for severe symptoms of ulceration in the digestive and urinary tracts and mouth and throat. It is used for ulcerative colitis with copious diarrhoea containing blood and mucus, and abdominal pains. Also, for severe bladder infections and urethritis with painful and frequent urination, the urine containing blood and mucus. There may be thick discoloured discharges containing pus. Throat and mouth symptoms include ulcerated tonsils covered with a white, pus-containing discharge, facial pain, exhaustion and secretion of excess saliva. Symptoms are worse in the evening and if the person walks about. They are also worse if the person eats fatty meals or acidic foods. Symptoms are better after breakfast and if the person rests.

Mercurius cyanatus

Mercuric cyanide

This homeopathic remedy is used to treat severe symptoms of diphtheria. The throat is extremely sore and the person finds swallowing and speech unbearable, and there is a covering of thick, greyish-white mucus. The person feels cold, and the skin has a blue-coloured tinge because of a lack of oxygen (cyanosis). The person may be on the verge of collapse.

Mercurius dulcis

Merc. dulc.; mercurous chloride, calomel, mercury chloride Hg_2Cl_2

This substance has laxative properties, and calomel was used as a purgative in medieval times. It is now used in the horticultural and agricultural industries as a constituent of certain insecticides and fungicides. Both *Mercurius dulcis* and *Mercurius corrosivus* are found in mineral deposits in the United States of America, Mexico, Germany and parts of central Europe. Merc. dulc. is a useful remedy for children suffering from glue ear and catarrhal problems. The child has swollen glands, and the nasal, ear and throat passages are clogged with discharges of thick, sticky mucus. Breathing may be noisy, and hearing is often affected. Symptoms are worse if the child is engaged in sport or physical exercise and also at night.

Mixed autumn moulds

MAP

This homeopathic remedy is derived from a mixture of three moulds—mucor, aspergillus and penicillum—and it is used to treat symptoms of hay fever that arise in the autumn. These symptoms include a runny nose and catarrh, itchy, red, watery eyes, sneezing and wheezing with a tight feeling in the chest. The usual time for symptoms to appear is in the early months of autumn, especially September.

Moschus moschiferus

Moschus; musk from the musk deer

Musk is a strong-smelling, aromatic secretion produced by the male musk deer in order to attract a female. The secretion has long been used in the production of perfume and has a long-lived effect. Samuel Hahnemann was concerned about the widespread use of musk-based scents, believing that the substance made people more susceptible to disease by weakening their natural immunity. The musk deer is a small deer found in countries of central Asia, inhabiting hilly or mountainous areas. Dried musk is used to prepare the homeopathic remedy, which is mainly given for hysterical, neurotic and emotional symptoms. Physical symptoms include giddiness and fainting, pallor and exhaustion and sweating. People suitable for this remedy have a tendency towards hypochondria and may feel that everyone is against them. They tend to talk incessantly and have hurried, clumsy movements. They tend to feel chilled, although one half of the body may seem cold and the other hot. Their exhaustion is worse for resting than for moving about, and all symptoms are aggravated by cool, fresh air and emotional upset or excitement. Symptoms improve after burping and for warm surroundings.

Murex

Purple mollusc

This homeopathic remedy is prepared from the body of the shellfish and is useful for menopausal symptoms of irregular bleeding. It is also used to treat emotional and hysterical symptoms and stress. A person suitable for this remedy dislikes being touched and especially having a medical examination.

Mygale lasiodora

Mygale las.; *Mygale avicularia*, *Aranea avicularia*, Cuban spider

This spider, which is a large variety native to Cuba, has a

highly poisonous bite used to immobilise its prey. If a person is bitten, the area becomes inflamed and discoloured, turning purple and green, and the effects spread outwards as the poison drains along the lymph vessels. The person experiences a high fever, tremor, chills, dry skin and mouth, severe anxiety and breathing difficulties and is very thirsty. The person fears that he or she will die. The homeopathic remedy is used to treat involuntary twitching and jerking of the muscles, which may be caused by nerve disorders such as various forms of chorea. The remedy is sometimes used to treat sexually transmitted venereal diseases. Symptoms are worse during the morning but improve when the person is sleeping.

Naja naja

Naja; *Naja tripudians*, venom of the cobra

The cobra, which has the habit of drawing itself erect and extending the skin below its neck to form a hood before it strikes, has long been both revered and feared. The snake is capable of shooting its venom into the eyes of its prey from a distance of six feet away, which causes blindness. The bite of the cobra may prove fatal, affecting the heart and lungs, causing collapse and death. The dried venom, which is bright yellow, is used to prepare the homeopathic remedy. It is used to treat left-sided symptoms, particularly of the heart, but also of the left ovary. Symptoms include crushing, choking pain as in angina, with the pain extending to the left shoulder and down the arm and hand. The pulse may be slow and the person feels breathless and oppressed. Ovarian pain may extend to the upper left-hand side of the body. Asthma that comes on after an attack of hay fever may be treated with Naja. The symptoms are made worse by lying on the left side, by cold draughts and following sleep. They are also aggravated by wearing tight, constricting clothing and drinking alcohol. For women, symptoms are worse following the monthly period.

Natrum carbonicum

Nat. carb.; sodium carbonate, soda ash

Sodium carbonate was once derived from the ashes of burnt seaweed but is now obtained from a chemical process. It is used industrially in the manufacture of detergents, soaps and glass-making. Sodium carbonate has various uses in conventional medicine, being used in creams and ointments to treat burns, eczema and other skin conditions. Also, it is used in preparations to clear up catarrh and vaginal discharge. The homeopathic remedy was investigated and proved by Hahnemann. It is used to treat a variety of skin disorders such as eczema, chapped, dry, sore skin, cold sores, moles, warts, corns and blisters. Also, for sore throats and catarrh, headache and indigestion. Symptoms are made worse by warm, humid weather, heat in any form, including being out in the hot sun. They are relieved by eating. People suitable for Nat. carb. have a sensitive, kind and intuitive nature, always ready to provide a sympathetic audience to others. They are devoted to their family and friends and give generously of themselves, endeavouring to be cheerful even when feeling unwell or depressed. They tend to be delicate and prone to digestive upsets, especially being intolerant of milk and dairy products. Ankles are another weak point, tending to be easily strained or sprained. Nat. carb. people are highly sensitive to music and are upset by noise and thunderstorms. They are soon exhausted by physical activity.

Natrum phosphoricum

Nat. phos.; sodium phosphate

Sodium phosphate occurs naturally in body cells and is one of the SCHUSSLER TISSUE SALTS (*see* GLOSSARY). It is involved in the regulation of acidity in body tissues and fluids, and in complex metabolic chemical processes utilising fatty acids. It is derived from a chemical reaction between sodium carbonate and phosphoric acid. It is a useful remedy for symptoms caused by an excess of lactic acid or uric acid. Excess lactic acid may be caused by a diet too rich in milk, dairy products or fatty foods. Also, there may be an excess of gastric or stomach acid, and this may be connected with eating too much sour food. The symptoms are those of acid indigestion with a sour taste in the mouth, wind and abdominal pains. An excess of uric acid is present in people suffering from gout with painful, inflamed stiff joints. Symptoms are made worse by thunderstorms and by eating fatty, sour or sweet foods and with physical exertion. They improve for being out in the fresh, clean air and for cool, airy surroundings. People suitable for this remedy tend to be refined and somewhat timid and prone to blush easily. They are easily exhausted but are inclined to be restless or slightly agitated. They do not accept advice readily and are prone to dissatisfaction and depression.

Natrum sulphuricum

Nat. sulph.; sodium sulphate, Glauber's salt, sal mirabile
Sodium sulphate is a naturally occurring substance within the body and is involved in the regulation of the salt/water balance in tissues and fluids. It is found in natural brines associated with salt lakes or can be manufactured by a chemical process. Sodium sulphate is used in industry in the manufacture of wood pulp and paper, glass, chemicals and detergents. It was investigated and proved by Schussler and is one of the tissue salts (*see* GLOSSARY). It is used in the treatment of liver disorders including jaundice, digestive complaints with indigestion and colicky pains, severe chesty conditions such as bronchitis and asthma, and blad-

der problems with urinary frequency. It is also used to relieve mental symptoms that arise after a head injury, such as depression or personality changes. Symptoms are made worse by damp, cold weather or surroundings and by lying on the back. The symptoms are worse at night and during the morning. Symptoms are relieved by cool, fresh, dry conditions and being out in the fresh air. Symptoms improve if the person changes position. People suitable for Nat. sulph. may either be very serious, keeping their emotions tightly controlled and putting up a front that may hide severe depression and suicidal thoughts. Or the depression may be more apparent, and they can become emotional on hearing music or contemplating art. These types are less repressed but still tend to suffer from depression. Nat. sulph. people are often somewhat materialistic and are very sensitive to damp weather with a tendency for asthma and chesty complaints with catarrh.

Nicotiana tabacum

Tabacum; tobacco

The tobacco plant derives its Latin name from Jean Nicot, a Portuguese diplomat who was an ambassador for France in South America during the 1500s. He brought tobacco to France in about 1560, but it had long been used by the Indian peoples. The plant has a hairy stem and leaves, giving off a narcotic odour. It contains nicotine, which is a powerful poison causing sickness and nausea, palpitations, sweating, headache and giddiness. It is now well established that smoking tobacco is a major cause of premature death. The homeopathic remedy is prepared from the fresh leaves of the plant and is given as a remedy for nausea and vomiting, such as in travel sickness, vertigo and disorders affecting the organs of balance in the ears. Symptoms are made worse by even slight movements such as turning the head, and for heat and tobacco smoke. They improve in cold surroundings and after vomiting.

Nitric acidum

Nitric ac; nitric acid, aqua fortis

This is a burning, extremely corrosive, clear liquid that gives off choking fumes that cause death by inhalation. Its industrial uses are mainly in the manufacture of agricultural fertilisers and high explosives. It has been used medicinally in extremely dilute form to treat severe infections and fevers, and to dissolve stones in the kidneys or bladder. It has been applied externally to the skin to burn away warts. Nitric acid is derived from a chemical reaction between sulphuric acid and sodium nitrate.

The homeopathic remedy is used to treat sharp, stabbing pains that may be intermittent in nature and are associated with piles, or haemorrhoids, anal fissure, ulcers in the mouth or on the skin, severe sore throat with ulceration, thrush infections and ulcers in the stomach or duodenum. Usually, the affected person suffers from broken, cracked skin with a tendency for ulcers and warts, and usually feels cold. The urine and other bodily secretions have a strong, pungent odour. Symptoms are worse for acidic fruits and drinks, milk, touch or pressure and movement. They are more severe at night and improve with heat and warm, dry surroundings. People suitable for Nitric ac. tend to be selfish, self-centred and apt to hold long grudges against others. They feel that everyone is against them but are themselves apt to fly into a rage and take offence very easily. They like to re-examine events and slights of the past and may be suspicious of other people. When ill, they are very fearful and worry that they may die.

Nux moschata

Nux mosch.; *Myristica fragrans*, nutmeg

The nutmeg tree grows mainly on an Indonesian island called Banda, which is one of the Molucca group, and also in the Far East and India. It was introduced to Constantinople (Istanbul) from India in about 540 AD and soon became widely used both for culinary, cosmetic and medicinal purposes. It was used to treat digestive upsets and headache and rheumatic pain. In herbal medicine, the remedy is given for sharper, clearer eyesight. In large doses, nutmeg produces hallucinogenic symptoms of drowsiness, giddiness and unsteadiness, with unco-ordinated movements and fainting. The homeopathic tincture is made from the inner seeds without their outer tough husks. The remedy is mainly given for mental and emotional disorders and digestive upsets. Symptoms include hysteria, agitation, excitement and exhaustion and drowsiness and confusion that may follow an epileptic attack or stroke. Also, for abdominal pains and indigestion, constipation and inflammation of the gastro-intestinal tract. People who benefit from this remedy have a need for fluids being somewhat dehydrated, but do not feel any great desire to drink. Symptoms are made worse by sudden changes in the weather and damp and cool conditions. They improve for being warm, wearing plenty of clothes and for high humidity.

Ocymum canum

Alfavaca, bush basil

This is a low-growing bushy plant that is a native of India and has a sweet scent. The homeopathic tincture is made from fresh leaves, and it is used as a remedy for renal colic and stones affecting the right kidney. The symptoms are pain and vomiting, a cloudy urine because of a deposit of reddish 'sand', and urinary frequency. There may be infection present and a sharp pain on passing urine, as in cystitis. The urine has a strong, pungent smell.

Oleander

Rose laurel

The fresh leaves are used to make the homeopathic remedy, which was first investigated and proved by Hahnemann. It is given for heart symptoms including palpitations, weakness, great anxiety and fainting. The person may feel giddy or be on the point of collapse. Also, for symptoms of gastroenteritis including diarrhoea, nausea and sickness and abdominal pains. The person often has sore, dry, chapped skin and is liable to suffer from depression, lack of concentration and clumsiness with a tendency for falls and even accidents. Physical symptoms that may benefit from this remedy include vertigo, headache, blurred vision, muscular weakness, and lack of co-ordination.

Oleum petrae

Petroleum

Petroleum, or liquid crude oil, is found trapped in oil-bearing rocks in the earth's crust and is derived from decayed organic material from the Carboniferous geological period. Petroleum is a vital fuel resource upon which people throughout the world are heavily reliant. In conventional medicine, petroleum jelly is used as an external treatment for minor skin abrasions. Purified petroleum is used to prepare the homeopathic remedy, which was first investigated and proved by Hahnemann and which is given for skin complaints. These include dry, cracked, chafed skin, particularly on the fingers, and eczema. These complaints are worse in cold weather, when the skin is subjected to chilling and heating. The remedy is also used for sickness, nausea and vomiting, especially as a result of travel sickness. There is a tendency for headaches to occur, especially in the back of the head. People who benefit from this remedy may be irritable because of having constantly inflamed, itchy, sore skin. They may fly into a rage and tend to have an excitable temperament. They dislike and are upset by fatty foods and their sweat has a strong odour. Symptoms are made worse by cold, windy weather, particularly during the winter months, and by thunderstorms. They improve with warmth and warm, dry weather and following a meal.

Onosmodium

False gromwell

The whole fresh parts of the green plant are needed to make the homeopathic remedy, which is used for mental symptoms including anxiety, tension and irritability. Also, for depression, lack of concentration and clumsiness, with a tendency for accidental and even accidents. Physical symptoms that may benefit from this remedy include vertigo, headache, blurred vision, muscular weakness and lack of co-ordination.

Ornithogalum umbrellatum

Star of Bethlehem

This remedy is used for severe, persistent, digestive upsets and is made from the whole green parts of the plant. There may be burning pains and regurgitation of stomach acid. The abdomen tends to be bloated with air, and there is flatulence. The person may suffer from depression and severe anxiety and is irritable and short-tempered with others. There is a tendency for peptic or duodenal ulcers to occur.

Oxalic acid

Sorrel acid, common wood sorrel, *Oxalis acetosella*

This remedy is derived from the leaves of sorrel, which have long had a culinary use. The leaves have a sour, sharp quality and can be used in place of vinegar. The plant itself is small and delicate and grows in Britain and other European countries. It produces delicate, white flowers shaped like little bells, which are veined with purple. Preparations made from the plant have cooling and diuretic properties. The homeopathic remedy is used for painful, rheumatic disorders, mainly affecting the left side of the body. The pains are severe and sharp, and the person becomes weak and cold. There is a tendency for small haemorrhages called petechiae to occur, which have the appearance of dark red spots beneath the skin. The person may have a tendency to bleed easily and to vomit blood.

Paeonia officinalis

Peony

This plant is well known in the British Isles as a pretty, deep pink garden flower, but it has been used medicinally since ancient times. It is believed to derive its name from a Greek physician called Paos, who, according to mythology, used it to cure the gods, including Pluto, of wounds sustained during the Trojan War. Many ancient superstitions and charms were connected with the plant, which was believed to have come from the moon and to have divine origins. The root of the peony has been used to prevent nightmare and epilepsy, as a cure for madness and to combat infection after childbirth. The fresh root, which is used to prepare both the herbal and homeopathic remedies, has antispasmodic, sedative and antiseptic qualities. In homeopathy, it is used as a remedy for itchy piles, or haemorrhoids, with discomfort and swelling. Also, it is used for sleep disturbance because of nightmares and indigestion and the need to sleep during the afternoons.

Papaver somniferum

Opium poppy, mawseed

The opium poppy is a native of Asia but is widely cultivated in other countries. In the wild, the poppy flowers are a pale mauve colour with a deeper purple spot at the base of the petals. Cultivated flowers have a variety of colours, from

white to red/purple. The unripened green seed capsules that develop at the base of the flowers are the part used in herbal medicine and homeopathy. An incision is made into the capsule, and a milky white juice is exuded that darkens as it dries. This is collected by scraping the capsules. The principal constituents of the opium juice are the alkaloids morphine and codeine, which are widely used in conventional medicine for their potent analgesic properties. Opium was used by the physicians of ancient Greece and Rome as a painkiller. It was probably introduced into India and hence to Europe by Arabian physicians. Dark grey poppy seeds, from the red/purple coloured flowers (called mawseed) are used in cooking and do not contain opium or morphine. They are also a constituent of bird seed. Opium has narcotic, sedative, hypnotic and antispasmodic properties. In homeopathy the remedy is used to treat symptoms of mental shock following a severe emotional shock or frightening experience. The symptoms may either be those of withdrawal and apathy, or of great agitation, excitement and sleeplessness with a greatly enhanced acute sense of hearing. It is also given for respiratory and breathing problems, constipation, alcohol withdrawal symptoms (delirium tremens) and following a stroke. Symptoms are worse for sleep and heat and improve with movement and exercise and in cool surroundings.

Pareira brava

Ice vine, velvet leaf

This climbing vine is a native species of Peru, Brazil and the West Indies and has very large leaves and flowers. It has a twisted, knotty root, and it is this part that is used to prepare the homeopathic remedy. Preparations made from the root have a stimulant effect on the kidneys and bowels and have diuretic and tonic properties. The homeopathic remedy is used for the treatment of urinary tract infections and disorders including cystitis, urethritis, urine retention and urinary frequency. There may be hot, burning pains on passing urine with abdominal pain or discomfort.

Paris quadrifolia

One berry, true love, herba Paris

This herbaceous, perennial plant flourishes in moist, shady conditions in woodlands throughout Europe and in Russia. A single stem is produced, which grows to a height of about ten inches or one foot, near the top of which are four pointed leaves. A single flower is produced in early summer, which is a whitish-green in colour and has an unpleasant rank smell. Later, a purple-black fruit is produced, which splits to release its seeds when ripe. The whole plant is used to prepare the homeopathic remedy, and it was first investigated and proved by Hahnemann. The plant is poisonous and has narcotic properties. If eaten in large quantities, it produces vomiting and diarrhoea, giddiness, dry throat, sweating and possibly convulsions and death. In homeopathy, it is used as an eye remedy for conjunctivitis and inflamed, irritated, itchy, watery eyes. Symptoms are mainly on the left side and the person is often excitable and talkative.

Parotidinum

The mumps nosode

This homeopathic remedy is derived from mumps-infected parotid salivary gland secretion. It is usually given as a preventative medicine to adults at risk of contracting mumps.

Passiflora incarnata

Passionflower, maypops

There are a number of species of passionflower, which gain their name from the resemblance of the blooms to the crown of thorns worn by Jesus. The plant produces large, sweet-scented flowers that are white or whitish-peach coloured with tinges of purple. Later, large berries with many seeds are produced, which are edible. The green parts of the plant are used to prepare herbal and homeopathic remedies. Preparations derived from the passionflower have sedative, narcotic and antispasmodic properties. In homeopathy, the remedy is used for convulsions, as in epilepsy, and also for illnesses in which there are severe spasms, such as whooping cough, asthmatic attacks and tetanus. Also, for serious mental disturbance, including delirium tremens resulting from alcoholism, and excited manic states.

Pertussin

Coqueluchin

This remedy is a nosode of whooping cough and is derived from material contaminated with the virus. It is given to treat the symptoms of whooping cough but also as a preventative measure for those at risk of contracting the disease.

Phellandrium aquaticum

Water fennel, fine-leaved water dropwort

This plant grows in ditches or on the banks of rivers near to the water; the lower parts may be submerged. The plant produces fruits that yield a yellow liquid from which the herbal and homeopathic remedies are derived. The preparations have expectorant and diuretic properties and are useful for treating chesty, bronchitic complaints. In homeopathy, the remedy is used for chest and respiratory disorders, with symptoms mainly on the right side. Conditions treated include bronchitis and emphysema with breathlessness, a severe cough and the production of thick mucus. Headache is another common symptom.

Phleum pratense

Timothy grass

This is a remedy for hay fever that is triggered by exposure to the pollen of flowering grasses. The person has the typical symptoms of watering, itchy eyes and running nose and sneezing. Breathlessness and asthma may also occur. The remedy is sometimes given to prevent the occurrence of an attack of hay fever.

Phosphoricum acidum

Phos. ac.; phosphoric acid

Phosphoric acid is a clear, crystalline substance that is obtained by a chemical process from a naturally occurring mineral, apatite. Apatite is rich in phosphate and occurs in various igneous (volcanic) and metamorphic rocks (ones altered by high temperatures and pressures) and mineral veins. Phosphoric acid has various industrial uses in the manufacture of fertilisers and detergents. It is used in the food industry as a flavouring for soft drinks and in the refining of white sugar. Also, it is used in the production of various pharmaceutical drugs. In conventional medicine it is used in the treatment of parathyroid gland tumours, acting to reduce blood calcium levels.

The homeopathic remedy was first investigated and proved by Hahnemann and is used to treat emotional and physical symptoms of apathy, exhaustion, listlessness and depression. These symptoms may arise from overwork or study or follow on after a debilitating illness that has caused dehydration. Other symptoms are a loss of appetite, feeling continually cold and shivery, dizziness, especially in the evening, and a feeling of pressure pushing downwards on the head. Phos. ac. is also given for growing pains in children or to those who suffer from sleep disturbance because of an awareness of sexual feelings. Symptoms are worse for cold, damp, draughty conditions and for loud noises. They improve following restful sleep and with warm surroundings.

Physostigma veneriosum

Calabar bean, chop nut, ordeal bean

This perennial climbing plant grows to a height of about 50 feet and is a native species of West Africa. It was introduced into Britain (and grown in the Botanical Gardens in Edinburgh) in 1846. It produces purple-coloured elongated flowers and later, dark brown seeds in pods about 6 inches in length. The seeds are extremely poisonous and were given as a test for witchcraft by West African peoples. If the accused person vomited after being forced to swallow the seeds, he or she was deemed innocent, but if death was the outcome then the accusation of being a witch was upheld. The poison causes depression of the central nervous system, slowing of the pulse and a rise in blood pressure, and death may follow because of respiratory collapse. Preparations made from the seeds are also miotic, causing a rapid contraction of the pupil of the eye, and its main use in herbal medicine is in the treatment of eye diseases. The ripe beans or seeds are used to prepare the homeopathic remedy, which is given for serious disorders in which there are muscular spasms. These include tetanus, meningitis and poliomyelitis. Also, for other disorders characterised by muscular and nervous degeneration or paralysis including Friedrich's ataxia, motor neurone disease and multiple sclerosis. The remedy may also be given for diarrhoea, vomiting, fever, sweating, prostration, and palpitations in which the pupils of the eye are very much contracted.

Phytolacca deccandra

Phytolacca; Virginian poke root, garget, reading plant, pocon, branching grape, pigeon berry

This plant is a native species of the United States and Canada, but is also found in Mediterranean countries, China and North Africa. It has a striking appearance and produces white flowers followed by clusters of shiny black berries. The orange-coloured fleshy root is the part used to prepare the homeopathic remedy, but both the root and berries are used in herbal medicine. Preparations derived from the plant have purgative, emetic and restorative properties. Native American Indians used poke root to cause vomiting and to encourage movement of the bowels and as a heart stimulant. It was also used as a remedy for skin disorders. Europeans used the plant to treat breast lumps and tumours and for mastitis (inflammation). In herbal medicine it is used to treat skin disorders, ringworm and scabies, chronic rheumatism, granular conjunctivitis (eye inflammation), ulcers and severe menstrual pain.

In homeopathy the remedy is given for small hard lumps or tumours in the breasts, which may be either benign or cancerous, and for mastitis. The breasts may be hot, swollen and painful to touch with stabbing pains. Also, it is used to treat severe sore throats and swallowing difficulty in which there is great pain, redness and inflammation. These symptoms may occur with tonsillitis, pharyngitis and diphtheria. The symptoms are made worse by swallowing, movement, hot drinks and in cold, damp draughty conditions. They improve with warmth and sunny, dry weather, cold drinks and having plenty of rest.

Picricum acidum

Picric acid

This poisonous substance is obtained by chemical reactions between nitric, sulphuric and carbolic acids. Since it was first investigated and proved for homeopathic use in 1868, it has been used to treat extreme exhaustion with mental and intellectual indifference and apathy. It usually occurs after an extended period of intense intellectual activity such as may occur among students cramming for exams. The person feels generally heavy and lethargic and is too tired to engage in conversation or to think clearly. Often, a numbing headache and aching eyes occur, or there may be a boil in the outer part of the ear. These symptoms may also arise as a result of grief. Symptoms are made worse with any physical or intellectual activity and in hot surroundings. They improve with rest and in cool conditions and if the weather is sunny but not hot.

Pilocarpus jaborandi, Pilocarpus microphyllus

Jaborandi

The drug known as Jaborandi is extracted from the leaves of *Pilocarpus*, which are shrubs native to Brazil. The leaves contain a volatile oil, and the most important active constituent of this is an alkaloid substance called pilocarpine. Preparations made from the leaves have diaphoretic properties, causing sweating, and are also stimulant and expectorant. Pilocarpine is mydriatic, causing contraction of the pupil of the eye. In herbal medicine, Jaborandi is used to treat diabetes, asthma, skin disorders such as psoriasis, catarrh and oedema (fluid retention). Also it is used as a tonic in preparations to stimulate new hair growth in the treatment of baldness. The homeopathic remedy is given for various eye and vision disorders, sweating because of the menopause or in hyperthyroidism (an overactive thyroid gland) and mumps.

Plantago major

Common plantain, broad-leaved plantain, waybread, ripple grass

This is a very familiar weed that grows throughout Britain and Europe and was introduced by colonists into the New World continents. The use of plantain in medicine goes back to ancient times, and it is described by Erasmus and Pliny. In Britain, plantain was an ingredient of many old remedies. It has been used in the past to treat wounds and external bleeding, for venomous bites and for disorders of the

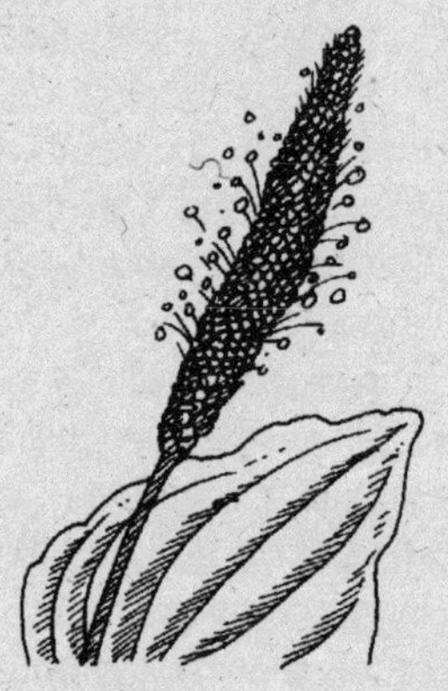

bowels and kidneys. It was used as a remedy for piles, or haemorrhoids, and to treat diarrhoea. Plantain is still used to treat these ailments in modern herbal medicine and homeopathy. The whole fresh plant is used to prepare the homeopathic remedy, which is sometimes used as the mother tincture. It is given for piles, toothache and tooth abscess and facial neuralgia. It is also used in the treatment of conditions such as diabetes, characterised by large quantities of urine being passed. Most symptoms occur on the left side and are worse for movement, cold and heat and draughts.

Platinum metallicum

Platinum

Platinum was discovered in South America during the 1700s. It is regarded as a very precious metal and is used to make jewellery. It is used in the electrical industry, in dentistry for fillings, and to make surgical pins to repair fractured bones. The homeopathic remedy is used almost entirely for female reproductive disorders that may have associated emotional problems. These include pain in the ovaries, spasm in vaginal muscles, making it difficult for the woman to have sexual intercourse (vaginisimus), heavy menstrual bleeding, absence of periods and genital itching. The woman may experience feelings of numbness, chilling and constriction of muscles and has a great fear of gynaecological examinations and procedures. Symptoms are made worse by touch and physical contact and by tiredness. They are worse in the evening but are relieved by being out in fresh clean air.

Women suitable for platinum set themselves and others extremely high standards of achievement that are not possible to attain. Hence they feel let down by apparent failures and tend to become depressed and irritable, feeling that the past was better than the present. They may become cynical and contemptuous of the efforts of others.

Plumbum metallicum

Plumbum met.; lead

Lead has been useful to humana for centuries and was used extensively by the Romans, especially to make pipes for plumbing systems. Lead continued to be mined and used throughout the ages, and has had many uses, e.g. in roofing, to make weights and lead shot, pencils, pottery glazes, paint and as an additive in fuel for vehicle engines. It has been known for some time, however, that lead is an insidious poison if present above a certain level in the human body. Early symptoms of poisoning are constipation that persists, weakness of muscles, pale skin and a blue line (because of lead sulphide) along the margin of gums and teeth. There is intellectual dullness and impairment and behavioural changes, and these are especially noticeable in children. Later, there are severe abdominal pains of a colicky nature, drooping wrists and feet, tremors, increasing muscular weakness and paralysis. Convulsions and lead encephalopathy affecting the brain may occur, leading to death if not diagnosed and treated.

The homeopathic remedy is used to treat long-term diseases of a sclerotic nature, i.e. leading to hardening of the affected tissues. These conditions include arteriosclerosis and atherosclerosis, Parkinson's disease and multiple sclerosis. Also for colic, constipation, muscular weakness and tremor and retention of urine. Symptoms are made worse by movement and are more severe at night. They improve with warmth and firm pressure or massage on the affected area. People suitable for Plumbum met. may have poor concentration and intellectual capabilities dulled by illness. They may have a poor memory and find it difficult to express themselves clearly. This intellectual impairment may make the person lethargic or short-tempered with others.

Podophyllum peltatum

Podophyllum; May apple, hog apple, American mandrake, duck's foot, wild lemon, racoonberry.

This herbaceous perennial plant is a native of the United States and Canada. The stalks grow to a height of about one or two feet and produce large, divided leaves and white flowers that have an unpleasant scent. Later, yellow fruits are produced that are edible although the leaves and roots are poisonous. The plant has a yellowish-brown rhizome and roots, and these are the parts used both in herbal medicine and homeopathy. Preparations made from the plant have purgative and emetic properties and act strongly on the liver and digestive organs. The plant was used by the native American peoples to eliminate parasitic worms and as a cure for deafness. The homeopathic remedy is given for digestive disorders such as vomiting and diarrhoea in gastroenteritis, gallstones, colicky pain and flatulence. There may be alternate bouts of diarrhoea and constipation. Symptoms are worse first thing in the morning and during hot weather. They are better for massaging the abdomen and for lying on the front.

Primula veris

Cowslip, herb Peter, key flower, mayflower, key of heaven, pargle, peggle

This familiar and pretty wild flower is common in shady woodlands in Europe and Great Britain. It produces delicate yellow flowers, and it is these that are used to prepare the herbal and homeopathic remedies. Preparations made from the plant have a sedative and antispasmodic effect. The flowers have been used to make cowslip wine, and the leaves were once valued as a salad vegetable. The homeopathic remedy is used for serious symptoms of high blood pressure and threatened stroke. These include confusion and giddiness, headache and a feeling of throbbing heat.

Prunus laurocerasus

Cherry laurel, cherry bay, common laurel

This fairly small evergreen shrub is a native species of Russia but also grows in Europe and some parts of Asia. It produces dark green shiny leaves and white flowers followed by clusters of black, cherry-like fruits. The fresh leaves are used to prepare the herbal and homeopathic remedies and give off a characteristic bitter almonds smell because of the presence of prussic acid. The shrubs are popular in gardens in Europe, having been first introduced in the late 16th century. The leaves are mainly used to produce cherry laurel water in herbal medicine, and preparations have a sedative effect. They are used for coughs and spasms, particularly whooping cough and asthma. The homeopathic remedy is used to treat severe symptoms of breathlessness and cyanosis (a blue tinge to the skin because of lack of oxygen in the blood) with a spasmodic cough. The symptoms are caused by serious disorders of the heart or lungs.

Psorinum

This remedy is derived from the fluid of scabies blisters and was first investigated and proved by Hahnemann. Hahnemann wrote extensively about the development of chronic diseases. He believed that in certain people the blisters produced in scabies were a manifestation of a deeper disorder. While the scabies blisters themselves might heal and disappear, this suppressed disease, or MIASM, still continued to cause disruption within the body and might even be passed on to subsequent generations. The symptoms or disorder associated with the scabies miasm are called psora and mainly affect the skin. The skin is dry, cracked and sore and there may be infections with pus-filled blisters. Also, digestive upsets, particularly diarrhoea and indigestion, exhaustion, depression and a pessimistic outlook on life are believed to be common manifestations of psora. The psorinum remedy is given to treat the symptoms described above and also for some respiratory ailments, especially hay fever, and general debility. Digestive ailments treated include irritable bowel syndrome and diverticulitis. Skin conditions such as eczema, acne, dermatitis, boils and ulceration may all respond to psorinum.

People suitable for this remedy are generally worried, pessimistic and gloomy, with a fear of all that may go wrong in life. They are very sensitive to cold and often feel chilled, even during the height of summer. They often experience a gnawing hunger and have a headache that is relieved by eating. They may feel that friends and family have deserted them. Symptoms are worse for cold winter weather and also for becoming too hot, either in bed or through physical exercise or wearing too many clothes. They improve in summer, with resting with the limbs spread out and with warm surroundings.

Ptelea trifoliata

Wafer ash, swamp dogwood, hop tree, wingseed, shrubby trefoil, ptelea

This small, shrubby tree, which grows to a height of six to eight feet, is a native species of the United States and Canada. The bark of the root is the part used to prepare remedies used in herbal medicine and homeopathy. The bark has a fairly pungent smell and a bitter taste and has a tonic effect, acting mainly on the liver and digestive organs. The homeopathic remedy is used mainly for liver disorders such as hepatitis and enlargement and tenderness. There is discomfort and heaviness in the region of the liver. Also, for digestive disorders, particularly indigestion, and rheumatism. All symptoms are mainly on the right side of the body and are made worse if the person lies on his or her right side.

Pyrogenium

Pyrogenium is a remedy introduced to homeopathy by Dr John Drysdale in 1880. It was a mixture of raw beef and water left to stand for three weeks. After straining, a straw-coloured liquid, called sepsin, was left, which, when mixed with glycerine, was called pyrogen. Dr Drysdale believed that pyrogen had profound effects upon the blood if taken in large amounts, causing septicaemia or blood poisoning. In modern homeopathy, the pyrogenium remedy is given for blood poisoning and septic conditions in which the healing process is rather slow. Characteristically, the person is feverish and has aching bones, a rapid pulse with feelings of heat and burning. The person is uncomfortable and restless and may have considerable pain if suffering from a septic condition such as an abscess. Symptoms are made worse by cold and draughts but improve with moving about.

Radium bromatum

Radium brom.; radium bromide

Radium bromide is derived from radium, which was discovered by Pierre and Marie Curie at the end of the 19th century. Radium is used in conventional medicine in radiotherapy for the treatment of cancer. It is obtained from the radioactive mineral uranite, which is also the main ore of uranium. Radium bromide is obtained by a chemical process from radium, and the homeopathic remedy is used to treat skin complaints in which there is itching and burning. Ailments include eczema, moles, skin ulcers, acne, skin cancer, rosacea (a red, flushed face and enlargement of the skin's sebaceous glands) and dry, chafed, sore skin. Also, for aching painful bones as in lumbago, rheumatic and arthritic disorders and bone cancer. Pains may move from one side of the body to the other, and symptoms are worse at night and on first moving after resting. They improve if the person lies down or moves about for a prolonged period. They are also better for lying down and for having a hot bath.

Rananculus bulbosus

Buttercup, bulbous buttercup, crowfoot, St Anthony's turnip, gold cup, frogsfoot

The familiar bright yellow buttercup is a familiar summer flower in Great Britain and other European countries. Small, bulbous swellings that resemble little turnips occur at the base of the stems. The plant can cause blistering and inflammation of the skin and has been used in a similar way to Cantharis (Spanish fly). The homeopathic remedy is used for skin irritation and blistering, as in shingles and eczema, and for rheumatism with hot, tearing pains. Also, for pleurisy with severe pains during breathing. All symptoms are made worse by cold and damp and if the person feels afraid. The person tends to be generally rundown and unwell.

Raphanus sativus

Black radish, black Spanish radish

There are many varieties of radish that are cultivated as salad vegetables. In herbal medicine, the juice obtained from the radish is used as a cure for gallstones and other stones or gravel. In homeopathy the remedy is used for abdominal flatulence and may be given post-operatively if there is sluggishness or some degree of paralysis of the digestive tract.

Rhatanhy

Krameria triandra, krameria root, Peruvian rhatany, rhantania

This low-growing shrub, which produces attractive large, red flowers, is a native species of Peru, growing in dry sandy soils in mountainous regions up to about 8,000 feet. The plant has strong roots, and it is these that are used to prepare the herbal and homeopathic remedies. Preparations made from the plant have astringent and tonic properties and have been used to treat anal fissure and haemorrhage, diarrhoea, urinary incontinence, and excessive menstrual bleeding. The homeopathic remedy is used to treat constipation with the development of painful haemorrhoids, or piles. The pains feel like glass splinters in the rectum and are very sharp. The person may have an odd sensation as though cold water is flowing over the molar teeth.

Rhododendron chrysanthemum

Rhododendron; yellow rhododendron, snow rose, rosebay

This low shrub or bush has a highly branched, reddish stem and grows to a height of about eighteen inches or two feet. The leaves are oval and resemble those of laurel. Large, attractive, golden yellow flowers are produced, and the plant is a native of the mountainous regions of Siberia, Asia and Europe. In herbal medicine the plant has long been used to treat rheumatic disorders and gout. The fresh leaves are used to prepare the herbal and homeopathic remedies. In homeopathy, the remedy is also used to treat gout, rheumatism and arthritis. Main symptoms are hot, painful swollen joints with severe pains. The remedy is additionally used for stabbing neuralgic pains around the eyes and in the face, pain in the testicles, high fever with confusion and delirium, and severe headaches. People who benefit from this remedy tend to have an anxious temperament. Symptoms are worse during the approach of a thunderstorm and at night. They are also made worse by standing still for a long period of time, by resting and at the start of movement. They improve with warmth and following a meal.

Rosa canina

Dog rose

The familiar dog-rose is an attractive bush producing pretty, delicately perfumed white or pink flowers in summer. Later, scarlet-coloured hips are produced containing the seeds that are used to make rose hip syrup. The hips have astringent and cooling properties and are a good source of vitamin C. They have been used in herbal medicine to treat diarrhoea, coughs and the coughing up of blood, as in consumption (tuberculosis), colic and kidney stones. In homeopathy, the remedy made from the ripe hips is used to treat disorders of the bladder and prostate gland, characterised by difficult and slow release of urine.

Rosmarinus officinalis

Rosemary, compass weed, polar plant, compass plant

This small, evergreen herb is a native of the arid, rocky hills along the Mediterranean coast but may also grow inland. It has been grown in Britain for centuries and has been important for both culinary and medicinal purposes. It was believed to affect the brain, strengthening the memory, and became associated with the virtues of remembrance, fidelity and friendship. It was included in bridal and funeral wreaths and flowers, burned as incense in religious festivals and believed to have magical properties. It was burnt or hung up as an antiseptic in sick rooms and hospitals, and strewn among clothes and linen to prevent attack by moths. Oil of rosemary was used externally to treat baldness, dandruff and gout in the hands and feet, and in wine for headaches, palpitations and dropsy (fluid retention or oedema). Oil of rosemary is obtained from the flowering sprigs or tops of the plant. The homeopathic remedy is used for memory loss and lack of concentration and for baldness.

Rumex crispus

Yellow dock, curled dock

This dock is commonly found on wasteland and along roadsides in the British Isles and has leaves that are curled and crisp at the edges. It grows to a height of about three feet and has large green leaves. The root is used in herbal medicine and has laxative and tonic properties. The homeopathic remedy is prepared from the whole flowering plant. It is used to treat itching skin conditions, nasal congestion with an abundance of thick, sticky catarrh, and diarrhoea and digestive disorders. Symptoms are made worse by cold and draughts and are better for warmth and heat.

Sabadilla officinarum

Sabadilla; *Asagraea officinalis*, cevadilla, cebadilla, *Veratum sabadilla*

These rushlike plants grow in the southern states of the United States, Mexico and Central America (Venezuela and Guatemala). The seeds are used to prepare herbal and homeopathic remedies, and these have been known in Europe since the 16th century. The preparations can be poisonous if taken internally, causing severe vomiting and diarrhoea. They were formerly used in Europe to kill intestinal parasitic worms and to eliminate lice. They were also used to treat rheumatism, gout and neuralgia. Sabadilla produces respiratory symptoms, resembling those of a cold, i.e. sneezing, running nose, watering, itchy eyes, coughing, headache and a painful sore throat. The homeopathic remedy is used to treat these symptoms and also to eliminate an infestation of threadworms. The symptoms are worse for cold and draughts and better for warmth and wearing warm clothes.

Sabal semilata

Sabal; the sabal palm, saw palmetto, palmetto scrub

This palm-like tree grows to a height of six to ten feet and has a crown of large, serrated leaves. It grows in the coastal regions of South Carolina and Florida and in southern California. Irregularly shaped, oval, dark brown berries are produced containing seeds, and these are a source of fatty oil. They are a valuable food source for wild animals, promoting weight gain. The fresh berries and seeds are used to prepare the remedies used in herbal medicine and homeopathy, and they have sedative, tonic and diuretic properties. The homeopathic remedy is mainly used to treat enlargement of the prostate gland, causing difficult, slow urination with sharp pains. Sexual intercourse may be painful, and there is general tiredness and loss of libido. Also, for inflammation of the testicles and breasts (mastitis) with heat, swelling and tenderness.

People who are suitable for sabal are afraid of going to sleep, and their symptoms are made worse by cold, damp conditions and the sympathy of others. Symptoms improve with warm, dry weather and surroundings.

Sabina cacumina

Savine; savine tops

The shrub or small evergreen tree *Juniperus sabina* is a native species of the northern states of North America and some European countries. This plant is grown in gardens in Britain, and the fresh spring growth is used to prepare herbal and homeopathic remedies. Preparations derived from the plant are irritant and poisonous in large doses and have powerful effects upon the uterus, causing bleeding. In herbal medicine the remedy is used externally for skin conditions, especially to encourage the drawing out of infection. In homeopathy the remedy is given for rectal and uterine bleeding with pains that may be stabbing or burning. Also, for cystitis, heavy menstrual periods and varicose veins.

Salvia officinalis

Sage, garden sage

Sage is a familiar garden herb that has been cultivated in Europe for many centuries. There are several varieties, but the wild form of sage is found in the warmer parts of Europe and along the Mediterranean coast. Sage has long been valued as a herb for flavouring food and to make a form of 'tea'. It has been used medicinally since ancient times and was used to treat liver diseases, wounds, ulcers and bleeding, especially the coughing up of blood, headache and rheumatic pains, throat infections, as a remedy for snake bites and to strengthen the brain and memory.

The homeopathic remedy is made from the fresh leaves and flowers, and preparations derived from sage have astringent and tonic properties and calming effects on the digestive organs. The remedy is used to treat hoarseness and sore throats, mouth ulcers or ulcerated throat and bleeding or infected gums.

Sanguinaria canadensis

Sanguinaria; red puccoon, blood root, coon root, sweet slumber, snakebite, Indian paint

This attractive, perennial plant is a native species of North America and Canada, growing in rich soils in woodlands. It produces beautiful, white flowers and has thick, bulbous fleshy roots containing orange-red sap. This juice was used by the native Indian peoples as dye for clothes and body paint. The root, green parts of the plant, fruit and seeds are used to prepare herbal and homeopathic remedies. The plant contains a potent alkaloid substance called sanguinarine, which forms colourless crystals. This is toxic in large doses, causing burning in the stomach with vomiting, thirst, giddiness, disturbed vision and possible collapse and death. In smaller doses the preparations have emetic and expectorant properties and also act on the uterus, promoting menstruation. In both herbal and homeopathy, the remedies are used for chest and respiratory ailments, including bronchitis, pharyngitis (inflammation of the pharynx), asthma and polyps (small, fleshy projections) in the nose or throat. Symptoms include dryness and soreness, thirst, chest pain that may extend to the right shoulder, and croup-like cough. Also, for whooping cough, colds and influenza, hay fever, severe migraine-like headaches with visual disturbance and rheumatic pains in the right shoulder. Symptoms often occur mainly on the right side and are worse if the person lies on that side of the body. They are made worse by cold, damp weather, touch and movement and by eating sweet foods. Symptoms improve in the evening and following sleep and if the person lies on the left side.

Sanicula aqua

Sanicula

Sanicula is a spring of water in Ottawa in Canada and Illinois in the United States of America. The water contains various salts and minerals that are themselves used to make homeopathic remedies. The sanicula remedy is mainly given to children with delicate stomachs and a tendency to suffer from constipation or diarrhoea after eating, vomiting and sickness, travel sickness and wetting the bed. Children who need this remedy are usually thin in spite of eating heartily and may have rapidly changing moods. Often there is a tendency for the head and feet to be hot and sweaty. Symptoms are made worse by downward, falling movements but improve if the child rests with little clothing or covering.

Secale comutum

Secale; ergot, spurred rye

The condition known as ergot is a form of fungus that grows on rye, wheat and various other grasslike cereals. The spores of the fungus germinate and grow on the stigmas and ovaries of the head of the grass. They form small, curved, black seed-like bodies (sclerotia, singular sclerotium) that eventually fall off when the ears of the cereal crop are ripe. The sclerotia are collected when immature before the grain is ripe to prepare the homeopathic remedy. Ergot has been known as a poison for many centuries. Cases of poisoning occurred because of eating foods made from contaminated cereals. Ergot contains several potent alkaloid substances, and symptoms of poisoning include burning pains, a crawling feeling on the skin, delirium, convulsions, gangrene, collapse and death. The substances have a powerful effect on the uterus and other smooth muscle, causing it to contract, and also on the central nervous system.

In modern homeopathy the remedy is used to treat spasms in the arteries, as in Raynaud's phenomena (numbness and blanching, redness and burning in fingers and toes), cramp-like pain in leg muscles, uterine pains and contractions leading to bleeding irregularities, and ineffective contractions during labour. The person has cold, numb skin but feels hot and burning inside. (In orthodox medicine, ergot is used to control postpartum haemorrhage following childbirth or abortion). Symptoms are worse for any form of heat or covering and better in cool, fresh air and surroundings.

Senecio aureus

Golden groundsel, life root, golden senecio, squaw weed

This perennial plant, which grows to a height of one or two feet, is a native of North America and Canada and also grows in Europe. It produces golden yellow flowers, and the whole plant is used to prepare the remedies used in herbal medicine and homeopathy. Preparations made from the plant have astringent and diuretic properties and also act on the uterus, chest and lungs. The homeopathic remedy is used for absent or suppressed periods that may be accompanied by pain, chesty catarrhal complaints, urinary problems such as kidney stones and cystitis, and bleeding problems, e.g. nosebleeds.

Smilax officinalis, Smilax medica

Sarsaparilla; red-bearded sarsaparilla, Jamaica sarsaparilla

The unusual name of this plant was derived from two Spanish words, *sarza* for 'bramble' and *parilla* for 'vine'. The plant has prickly, thorny stems and is a native of

Central and South America. It is thought to have been exported via Jamaica to Europe, but it does not grow in the West Indies. It was once used as a treatment for syphilis, and smoke from the burning plant was considered beneficial in the treatment of asthma. Preparations made from the plant have diuretic and tonic properties and promote perspiration. The fresh root is used to prepare the herbal and homeopathic remedies. In homeopathy sarsaparilla is used to treat bladder, kidney and urinary disorders, especially kidney stones causing renal colic and cystitis. There is a frequent need to urinate, although only small amounts may be passed, and sharp burning pains. The urine frequently appears cloudy, containing small deposits or stones. There may be a slight degree of incontinence of urine, especially if sitting down. The remedy is also used for rheumatism with pains that are worse at night and in cold, damp, draughty conditions. Also, for eczema and dry skin with painful deep cracks and fissures. People who benefit from this remedy feel cold and have a tendency to have dry scaly skin and spots. Skin conditions are worse in the months of spring. Symptoms are worse at night and in cold, damp, draughty conditions. They improve if the person is standing and uncovers the chest and neck.

Solanum dulcamara

Dulcamara; woody nightshade, scarlet berry, bittersweet, felonwort, felonberry, violet bloom

This rambling, trailing plant grows over bushes and hedges, extending for a considerable distance and supported by other plants. It is a native species of many European countries, including Britain. The young stems of the plant are green and furry, but they become more woody and smooth with age. The plant produces purple-blue flowers and, later, berries that are bright red when ripe. The stems taste bitter at first if chewed and then sweet (hence, bittersweet). Felon is an old name for a whitlow (an abscess on a finger or toe) and the name felonwort refers to the fact that the plant was used to cure these. Woody nightshade has a long history of medicinal use going back to ancient times. It has been used to treat a wide variety of disorders, especially skin complaints, asthma and chesty, catarrhal conditions, rheumatism and absent menstruation. The young shoots and twigs, leaves and flowers are used to prepare the homeopathic remedy. This is given for ailments that are made worse, or are brought on, by exposure to cold and damp or sudden cooling, including colds and coughs, catarrhal complaints and conjunctivitis. Also, for skin conditions such as eczema, itchy rashes, ringworm, nettle rash (urticaria) and warts. Symptoms are worse for cold, damp weather and changes of temperature. They improve with exercise, movement, warmth and heat.

Solidago virgaurea

Golden rod, woundwort, Aaron's rod, solidago

This familiar garden plant grows in Europe, Asia and North America. It produces green leaves and golden yellow flowers and has long been valued as a remedy for kidney and urinary disorders, especially kidney stones. The green parts are used to prepare the homeopathic remedy, which is used to treat problems of urine retention and lack of urination and renal colic.

Spigelia anthelmia

Spigelia; pink root, annual worm grass

This perennial plant is a native of the northern countries of South America and the West Indies, and a related type, *Spigelia marylandica*, grows in some states of North America. It was used by the native Indian peoples to expel intestinal parasitic worms, and is narcotic and a potent poison if taken in large amounts. The fresh plant has an unpleasant smell and is gathered and dried to prepare the homeopathic remedy, which is given especially for left-sided symptoms and particularly heart disorders. These include angina and coronary artery disease with severe pain. Also given for neuralgia, left-sided headache and migraine, iritis (inflammation of the iris of the eye), all of which are accompanied by sharp pains. People who benefit from this remedy have a phobia about long, pointed, sharp objects, e.g. needles. Symptoms are worse for lying on the left side, cold air, touch and movement, and during the approach of a thunderstorm. They improve with warm, dry conditions, lying on the right side, in the evening and for having the head raised when resting.

Spongia tosta

Spongia; natural sponge

Natural sponge has been used since the early Middle Ages to treat the enlargement of the thyroid gland, known as goitre, that results from a deficiency in iodine. The condition may result from a dietary lack of iodine or by some disorder of metabolism or of the thyroid gland itself. In more recent times, scientists discovered that sponges are naturally rich in iodine. Roasted sponge is used to prepare the homeopathic remedy, which is used to treat thyroid gland disorders and goitre. There may be symptoms of palpitations, flushing, sweating, breathlessness, heat intolerance, anxiety and nervousness. Also, for heart disorders, including an enlarged heart or disease of the valves. Symptoms include palpitations, pain, breathlessness, exhaustion and a feeling of being crushed by a heavy weight. The person may be flushed and anxious with a fear of death. The Spongia remedy is useful in the treatment of a hoarse, dry sore throat, as in laryngitis, and particularly where respiratory illnesses such as tuberculosis are associated with the family. Symptoms are worse for movement, touch, trying to talk and for cold drinks and cold surroundings. They improve with warmth and warm meals and drinks, and for sitting propped up. People suitable for Spongia are often thin with a fair complexion and light-coloured hair.

Stannum metallicum

Stannum met.; tin

Tin is obtained from the mineral cassiterite, which occurs as dark-coloured crystals in such rocks as pegmatites and granites and in the alluvial deposits of streams and rivers. Tin is a soft, silver-coloured metal that has long been useful to humankind and has had many industrial uses. Medicinally, it was once given to expel intestinal tapeworms. In modern homeopathy, the remedy is used for severe catarrhal chest complaints, including bronchitis, laryngitis, asthma and inflammation of the windpipe (tracheitis). There is a thick, yellowish catarrh and a hoarse, dry cough. The person is sometimes weak and debilitated, suffering from loss of weight and exhaustion with associated depression and weepiness. The remedy is also given for neuralgic pain and headache, particularly on the left side. The pains may have a gradual onset and also be slow to disappear. Symptoms are made worse if the person lies on his or her right side and drinks warm fluids. They improve for coughing up catarrh and for firm pressure on the painful part.

Sticta pulmonaria

Sticta; lungwort, oak lungs, lung moss, Jerusalem cowslip

This plant, which is familiar in gardens in Great Britain and other European countries, has rough, oval green leaves speckled with white, reminiscent of lungs. The stalks grow to a height of about one foot, and the flowers are a pinky-red at first but purply-blue when fully open. Preparations of the plant have astringent properties and act on the mucous membranes of the respiratory tract. The homeopathic remedy is prepared from the whole fresh plant and is used to treat colds, asthma, lung inflammation and rheumatic disorders. The catarrh is difficult to cough up and persistent. Symptoms are worse at night and for cold, damp conditions. They are worse for lying down and better for warmth.

Strophanthus kombe, Strophanthus hispidus

Kombé seeds

These climbing plants are native to tropical parts of East Africa. The name is derived from two Greek words, *strophos*, 'rope' or 'twisted cord', and *anthos*, 'flower'. They produce seeds that are extremely poisonous, and the poison was used on arrows for hunting by African tribal peoples. The most active constituents are a glucoside substance called strophanthin and an alkaloid, inoeine. Preparations made from the seeds have a similar effect to digitalis, and are used to treat heart and circulatory disorders. The homeopathic remedy is used to treat palpitations, irregular heartbeat and breathlessness. It is a useful remedy for those whose health has been compromised by smoking or drinking alcohol.

Sulphuric acid

This remedy is used for mental exhaustion and depression, the person being restless and agitated. There is a tendency for skin problems to occur, including ulcers and boils. Other symptoms include mouth ulcers, bleeding gums and depression.

Symphoricarpus racemosa

Snowberry, wolf berry, coal berry, wax berry

Preparations made from this North American plant have

emetic and purgative properties. The homeopathic remedy is used for cases of severe vomiting and nausea, including morning sickness in pregnancy. There is a loss of appetite and there may also be a loss of weight.

Syphilinum

This remedy is derived from material obtained from a syphilitic lesion. Syphilis is a serious sexually transmitted bacterial disease that has plagued humankind for centuries. Hahnemann believed that syphilis was one of three main MIASMS, having an inherited element from earlier generations affected with the illness. The homeopathic remedy is used to treat chronic ulcers and abscesses, especially in the genital area. Also for menstrual pains, neuralgia, varicose ulcers, constipation and inflammation of the iris of the eyes (iritis). The person may experience pain in the long bones and have weak teeth. Symptoms are worse for great heat or cold, at night, near the sea and during a thunderstorm. They improve with gentle walking and through the day and for being in a mountainous region.

People suitable for this remedy tend to be anxious and on edge, with nervous mannerisms such as exaggerated blinking or a muscular twitch or tic. They may show obsessive behaviour, such as a need to recheck constantly on something or to keep on washing their hands. They may find it difficult to concentrate and have a poor memory. They may have a problem with alcohol, drugs or smoking.

Tammus communis

Black bryony, blackeye root

This poisonous climbing plant is common in hedges, copses and open woodlands in the British Isles. It has heart-shaped leaves and white flowers, with bright red berries produced in the autumn. The plant has a dark-coloured root that is the part most often used in herbal medicine and homeopathy. Preparations made from the plant have diuretic and blistering properties and are helpful for clearing the discoloration of a bruise (hence blackeye root). The homeopathic remedy is used to treat chilblains with soreness, redness, inflammation and itching.

Terebinthinae oleum

Terebinth; turpentine

Turpentine is obtained from pine and other coniferous trees in the form of an oily, aromatic resin. It has many industrial uses, especially as a cleaning agent, in paint strippers and thinners and in products containing pine oil. It causes burning if swallowed and produces vomiting and diarrhoea. It also causes external burning and blistering if applied to the skin, and choking, sneezing and coughing if the fumes are inhaled. It was once used in the treatment of genital infections, including gonorrhoea. The homeopathic remedy is used to treat similar types of infection involving inflammation and infection of the bladder and kidneys. These include cystitis with frequent urination, blood in the urine and burning pains, and kidney inflammation with stabbing back pains. The urine is usually cloudy or contains blood and may have a strong smell. Also, for other forms of kidney disease with symptoms of puffiness because of retention of fluid (oedema). Symptoms are worse at night and in cold, damp, draughty conditions. They are better for walking about in fresh clean air and for warmth.

Teucrium marum venum

Teucrium mar. ver.; cat thyme, marum

This strongly aromatic plant is a native of Spain but grows in many countries throughout the world. It has branching stalks and forms a bush or shrub about two to four feet in height. The small, oval leaves are sage green in colour and slightly furred, and the flowers are an attractive deep pink. Both flowers and leaves have a pungent aromatic smell, especially when rubbed. The plant has stimulant and astringent properties and has long been used in herbal medicine for a variety of disorders. All the fresh parts of the plant are used to prepare the homeopathic remedy, which is used to treat polyps, which are small growths or tumours on mucous membranes. These may occur in the rectum, bladder or nasal passages. Also, the remedy is used for conditions producing thick catarrh that is persistent and difficult to eliminate. The remedy may be given to treat threadworm infestation in children. Symptoms are worse for cold, damp conditions and sudden weather changes. Also, if the person becomes hot and sweaty in bed. Symptoms improve for being out in the cool, fresh clean air.

Theridion curassavicum

Orange spider of Curaçao and other parts of the West Indies

This is a small spider about the size of a pea that has a body covered with orange spots. There is a larger yellow spot on its under surface, and it is particularly found in Curaçao. It has a poisonous bite and causes unpleasant symptoms of tremor, chilling, sweating, fainting and great anxiety. The whole spider is used to prepare the homeopathic remedy, which was first investigated and proved in the early 1830s by Dr Constantine Hering. The remedy is used to treat ailments of the spine and nerves and bone disorders. All these ailments are very sensitive to movement, vibration and noise, which set off sensations of great pain. Disorders treated include Ménière's disease, a disease of the inner ear with deafness and tinnitus (ringing in the ear) with symptoms of vertigo, nausea and vomiting. Also, toothache, degeneration of bones and spine with inflammation and pain, morning sickness, travel sickness, vertigo, severe headache, chills and fainting. Symptoms are made worse by closing the eyes, by any kind of movement or vibration, bending, touch and during the night. They improve for rest with the eyes open and with warmth and quiet surroundings.

Trillium erectum, Trillium pendulum

Bethroot, Indian balm, birthroot, Indian shamrock, lamb's quarters, wake-robin

Plants belonging to this group are all native species of North America. *Trillium erectum*, which flourishes in rich, moist soils in woodlands and grows to a height of between one foot and sixteen inches, produces white flowers. Preparations made from the plant have astringent, antiseptic and tonic properties and were used by the native Indian peoples for childbirth and haemorrhage, especially from the womb. The homeopathic remedy is used to treat heavy bleeding from the womb, which may be associated with fibroids or the menopause. It may be given to prevent an early threatened miscarriage.

Tuberculinum koch, Tuberculinum bovum

Dead, sterile tuberculous tissue derived from cattle or human beings

This remedy was extensively investigated and researched

by Dr Compton Burnett in the late 1800s, following an earlier discovery by Dr Robert Koch, that dead tuberculous material was effective in the prevention and treatment of tuberculosis. The homeopathic remedy is given for chronic conditions characterised by wasting, pallor, a persistent racking cough, drenching sweats at night and pains in the left lung. The glands in the neck are enlarged, and the whites of the eyes (sclera) may appear slightly blue.

Symptoms are erratic and may move about. Often there is a family history of tuberculosis or other severe respiratory disorder such as asthma. People who benefit from this remedy are usually thin, fair-haired and blue-eyed, prone to colds and chest ailments and lacking physical strength and stamina. They tend to be restless, seeking constant change in their personal life and surroundings, yearning for excitement, travel and new romantic attachments. They may be afraid of dogs or cats and enjoy milk and the taste of smoked foods.

Valerian officinalis

Great wild valerian; all-heal, setwall, capon's tail

Valerian species grow throughout Europe and northern Asia, and *Valerian officinalis* flourishes in marshy, wet ground in ditches and near rivers and streams. The stems reach a height of three to four feet, producing dark green leaves and light pink flowers. The rhizome or root is the part used in herbal medicine and homeopathy, and the plant has a long history of medicinal use. It was valued so highly in the Middle Ages as to be given the name all-heal, while its Latin name may be derived from *valere*, meaning 'to be in health'. Preparations made from the plant have powerful effects on the central nervous system, acting as sedatives and antispasmodics. The homeopathic remedy is given for excitable, mental symptoms including agitation and restlessness. Also, for muscular spasms, hysteria, headache and pains that may move from one part to another. The person may suffer from sleeplessness, headaches, diarrhoea and restlessness with gnawing hunger and nausea.

Veratum album

Verat. alb.; white hellebore

This plant grows throughout Europe, although not in the British Isles, and produces a creamy-white flower. The rhizome or root is the part used in herbal medicine and homeopathy, and it is extremely poisonous. If swallowed it causes diarrhoea and vomiting and may result in collapse, convulsions and death. Preparations made from the plant have irritant and cardiac depressant properties. There is a long history of medicinal use going back to the time of Hippocrates, and the remedy was investigated and proved for homeopathy by Hahnemann during the late 1820s.

The homeopathic remedy is used for severe conditions of collapse and shock in which there is pallor, dehydration, chilling and possibly cyanosis (a blue tinge to the skin because of a lack of oxygen in the blood and tissues). The person may be cold with clammy skin because of sweating. Also, for diarrhoea, severe throbbing headache and mental symptoms of extreme agitation or severe depression, suicidal feelings, mania and aggression. It may be given for severe cramping menstrual pain or cramp during pregnancy leading to fainting, and collapse because of mental shock or trauma. Symptoms are made worse by movements and cold drinks, and also during the night. They improve with warmth, heat and hot meals and drinks. They are also better for rest and lying down.

Viburnum opulus

Guelder rose, high cranberry, dog rowan tree, cramp bark, snowball tree, rose elder

The guelder rose is a bush or small tree found in copses

and hedges in England, Europe and North America. It produces abundant heads of white flowers and, later, bright red berries that have a bitter taste. The bark, which contains a bitter glucoside substance called viburnine, is used to prepare remedies in herbal medicine and homeopathy. Preparations of the bark are very effective in the relief of cramp-like pains and spasms. The homeopathic remedy is used to treat menstrual cramps, pain in the ovaries at ovulation and prevention of early threatened miscarriage.

Vinca minor

Lesser periwinkle

This trailing plant grows in Great Britain and other European countries, producing dark-green leaves and purply-blue flowers. Periwinkles have a long history of use in herbal medicine and were used to treat bleeding, cramps, piles and skin inflammations. There are also

many ancient superstitions attached to the plant, and it was believed to ward off evil spirits. Preparations made from the plant have astringent and tonic properties. In homeopathy it is used for heavy menstrual bleeding and haemorrhage and for inflammations of the scalp.

Viola tricolor

Wild pansy, love-lies-bleeding, love-in-idleness, hearts-ease, and many other country names

This pretty flower is abundant throughout the British Isles, with rounded green leaves and purple, yellow and white flowers. The whole plant is used to prepare herbal and homeopathic remedies that have a long history of medicinal use. The plant has been used to treat a wide variety of ailments, including asthma, epilepsy, skin disorders, convulsions, heart and blood disorders. Preparations made from the plant have diuretic properties. In homeopathy, the remedy is used for skin conditions such as infected eczema or impetigo. There is a thick pus-containing discharge and crusts and scabs on the skin. Also, the remedy is used to treat bed-wetting and urinary incontinence.

Vipera communis

Venom of the adder or viper

This attractively patterned snake is a greyish colour with a dark zig-zag pattern down the length of its back. Its bite is painful but rarely serious, causing swelling, inflammation and bleeding in the veins, which then become enlarged. The homeopathic remedy made from the venom of the snake, is used to treat phlebitis and varicose veins and ulcers with swelling, inflammation and pain. The leg feels heavy, as though it might burst. Symptoms are worse for touch, pressure or tight clothing and are relieved by raising the affected part.

Viscum album

Mistletoe

This parasitic plant grows in the British Isles and throughout Europe, trailing over fruit and other trees. It produces white berries that ripen in December, but the leaves and twigs are used to prepare the remedies for herbal medicine and homeopathy. Preparations derived from the plant act on the central nervous system and have tonic, antispasmodic and narcotic properties. It has been used to treat

epilepsy, spasms and haemorrhage. Many ancient superstitions are attached to mistletoe, which was a sacred plant for the Druids. In homeopathy, the remedy is used as a last resort to treat extreme conditions of collapse, weak pulse and respiration and low blood pressure.

Vitex agnus castus

Agnus castus; chaste tree; monk's pepper, wild lavender

This aromatic shrub is a native plant of the shores of the Mediterranean and also grows in other part of Europe and North America. It has flexible fine twigs that are used to weave baskets, dark green leaves and fragrant flowers. Dark, purply-red berries are produced containing seeds, and these are used to prepare herbal and homeopathic remedies. The plant was associated with chastity by the ancient Greeks. The plant was used to treat muscular weakness and paralysis and is used in herbal medicine to stimulate hormone production during the menopause. The homeopathic remedy is given for menopausal symptoms and for physical disorders arising from alcohol or drug abuse or sexual excess. Symptoms may include fatigue, depression, loss of sexual desire, apathy and inability to concentrate. Also for postnatal depression with loss of libido and drying up of the breast milk. Symptoms are worse in the morning and for exercise and movement and are relieved by firm pressure on an affected part.

Zincum metallicum

Zinc. met.

Zinc is an essential trace element in the human body, being a constituent of digestive enzymes and essential for normal growth. Zinc is used in conventional medicine as a constituent of creams and ointments for a variety of skin complaints. It is also taken internally for some nervous complaints, spasms and neuralgia. The homeopathic Zinc. met. remedy is prepared from zinc sulphide and is used for conditions of restlessness, agitation and nervous twitching. The person is usually suffering from great mental and physical exhaustion and is irritable and highly sensitive to the least noise, interruption or touch. Symptoms are worse for suppression of natural discharges (e.g. by using a suppressant remedy in the case of a cold). Also, they are made worse by noise, touch, vibration and alcoholic drinks, particularly wine. Symptoms improve when natural body functions take place and are not suppressed.

Glossary of Terms used in Homeopathy

aggravations a term first used by Dr Samuel Hahnemann to describe an initial worsening of symptoms experienced by some patients, on first taking a homeopathic remedy, before the condition improved. In modern homeopathy this is known as a *healing crisis*. To prevent the occurrence of aggravations, Hahnemann experimented with further dilutions of remedies and, in particular, vigorous shaking (SUCCUSSING) of preparations at each stage of the process.

allopathy a term first used by Dr Samuel Hahnemann meaning 'against disease'. It describes the approach of conventional medicine, which is to treat symptoms with a substance or drug with an opposite effect in order to suppress or eliminate them. This is called the 'law of contraries' and is in direct contrast to the 'like can cure like', the 'law of similars' or *similia similibus curentur* principle, which is central to the practice of homeopathy.

centesimal scale of dilution the scale of dilution used in homeopathy based on one part (or drop) of the remedy in 99 parts of the diluent liquid (a mixture of alcohol and water).

classical the practice of homeopathy based on the work of Dr Samuel Hahnemann and further developed and expanded by other practitioners, particularly Dr Constantine Hering and Dr James Tyler Kent.

constitutional prescribing and constitutional types the homeopathic concept, based on the work of Dr James Tyler Kent, that prescribing should be based on the complete make-up of a person, including physical and emotional characteristics, as well as on the symptoms of a disorder.

decimal scale of dilution the scale of dilution used in homeopathy based on one part (or drop) of the remedy in nine parts of the diluent liquid (a mixture of alcohol and water).

healing crisis the situation in which a group of symptoms first become worse after a person has taken a homeopathic remedy, before they improve and disappear. The healing crisis is taken to indicate a change and that improvement is likely to follow. It is usually short-lived (*see also* AGGRAVATIONS).

homeopathy the system of healing based on the principle of 'like can cure like' and given its name by Samuel Hahnemann. The word is derived from the Greek *homeo* for 'similar' and *pathos* for 'suffering' or 'like disease'.

laws of cure, law of direction of cure three concepts or 'laws' formulated by Dr Constantine Hering to explain the means by which symptoms of disease are eliminated from the body.

(1) Symptoms move in a downwards direction.
(2) Symptoms move from the inside of the body outwards.
(3) Symptoms move from more important vital organs and tissues to those of less importance.

Hering was also responsible for the view in homeopathy that more recent symptoms disappear first before ones that have been present for a longer time. Hence symptoms are eliminated in the reverse order of their appearance.

materia medica detailed information about homeopathic remedies, listed alphabetically. The information includes details of the symptoms that may respond to each remedy, based on previous research and experience. Details about the source of each remedy are also included. This information is used by a homeopathic doctor when deciding upon the best remedy for each particular patient and group of symptoms.

miasm a chronic constitutional weakness that is the after-effect of an underlying suppressed disease that has been present in a previous generation or earlier in the life of an individual. The concept of miasm was formulated by Samuel Hahnemann who noted that some people were never truly healthy but always acquired new symptoms of illness. He believed that this was because of a constitutional weakness that he called a miasm, which may have been inherited and was caused by an illness in a previous generation. These theories were put forward in his research writings entitled *Chronic Diseases*. Three main miasms were identified, PSORA, SYCOSIS and SYPHILIS.

modalities a term applied to the responses of the patient, when he or she feels better or worse, depending upon factors in the internal and external environment. These are unique from one person to another, depending upon the individual characteristics that apply at the time, although there are common features within each constitutional type. Modalities include responses, fears and preferences to temperature, weather, foods, emotional responses and relationships, etc, which all contribute to a person's total sense of wellbeing. Modalities are particularly important when a person has symptoms of an illness in prescribing the most beneficial remedy.

mother tincture (symbol O) the first solution obtained from dissolving a substance in a mixture of alcohol and water (usually in the ratio of 9/10 pure alcohol to 1/10 distilled water). It is subjected to further dilutions and SUCCUSSIONS (shakings) to produce the homeopathic remedies.

nosode a term used to describe a remedy prepared from samples of infected diseased tissue, often to treat or prevent a particular illness. They were first investigated by Wilhelm Lux, not without considerable controversy. Examples are *Medorrhinum* and *Tuberculinum*.

organon *The Organon of Rationale Medicine*. is one of

the most important works of Samuel Hahnemann, published in Leipzig in 1810, in which he set out the principles and philosophy of modern homeopathy. The *Organon* is considered to be a classic work and basic to the study of homeopathy.

polycrest a remedy suitable for a number of illnesses, disorders or symptoms.

potency the dilution or strength of a homeopathic remedy. Dr Samuel Hahnemann discovered that by further diluting and SUCCUSSING (shaking) a remedy, it became more effective or potent in bringing about a cure. It is held that the process of diluting and shaking a remedy releases its innate energy or dynamism, even though none of the original molecules of the substance may remain. Hence the greater the dilution of a remedy, the stronger or more potent it becomes. Hahnemann called his new dilute solutions 'potentisations'.

potentiate the release or transfer of energy into a homeopathic solution by succussing or vigorous shaking of the mixture.

principle of vital force 'vital force' was the term given by Samuel Hahnemann to the inbuilt power or ability of the human body to maintain health and fitness and fight off illness. Illness is believed to be the result of stresses, causing an imbalance in the vital force, which assail all people throughout life and include inherited, environmental and emotional factors. The symptoms of this 'disorder' are illness and are held to be the physical indications of the struggle of the body's vital force to regain its balance. A person with a strong vital force will tend to remain in good health and fight off illness. A person with a weak vital force is more likely to suffer from long-term, recurrent symptoms and illnesses. Homeopathic remedies are believed to act upon the vital force, stimulating it to heal the body and restore the natural balance.

provings the term given by Samuel Hahnemann to experimental trials he carried out to test the reactions of healthy people to homeopathic substances. These trials were carried out under strictly controlled conditions (in advance of the modern scientific approach), and the symptoms produced, the results, were meticulously recorded. Quinine was the first substance that Hahnemann investigated in this way, testing it initially on himself and then on close friends and family members. Over the next few years he investigated and proved many other substances, building up a wealth of information on each one about the reactions and symptoms produced. After conducting this research, Hahnemann went on to prescribe carefully the remedies to those who were sick. Provings are still carried out in modern homeopathy to test new substances that may be of value as remedies. Usually, neither the prescribing physician nor those taking the substance—

the 'provers'—know the identity of the material or whether they are taking a placebo.

psora one of three MIASMS identified by Samuel Hahnemann, believed to be because of suppression of scabies (an itchy skin infection caused by a minute burrowing mite). Psora was believed to have an inherited element or to be because of suppression of an earlier infection in a particular individual.

Schussler tissue salts Wilhelm Heinrich Schussler was a German homeopathic doctor who introduced the biochemic tissue salt system in the late 1800s. Schussler believed that many symptoms and ailments resulted from the lack of a minute, but essential, quantity of a mineral or tissue salt. He identified twelve such tissue salts that he regarded as essential and believed that a cure could be obtained from replacing the deficient substance. Schussler's work was largely concentrated at the cell and tissue level rather than embracing the holistic view of homeopathy.

similia similibus curentur the founding principle of homeopathy that 'like can cure like' or 'let like be treated by like', which was first put forward by Hippocrates, a physician of ancient Greece. This principle excited the interest of Paracelsus in the Middle Ages, and was later restated and put into practice by Hahnemann with the development of homeopathy.

simillimum a homeopathic remedy that in its natural, raw state is able to produce the same symptoms as those being exhibited by the patient.

succussion vigorous shaking of a homeopathic remedy at each stage of dilution, along with banging the container holding it against a hard surface causing further release of energy.

sycosis one of the three major MIASMS identified by Samuel Hahnemann and believed to result from a suppressed gonorrhoeal infection. Sycosis was believed to have an inherited element or to be because of suppression of an earlier infection in a particular individual.

syphilis the third of the three major MIASMS identified by Samuel Hahnemann believed to result from a suppressed syphilis infection. Syphilis was believed to have an inherited element or to be because of suppression of an earlier infection in a particular individual.

trituration the process, devised by Samuel Hahnemann, of rendering naturally insoluble substances soluble so that they can be made available as homeopathic remedies. The process involves repeated grinding down of the substance with lactose powder until it becomes soluble. The substance usually becomes soluble at the third process of trituration. Each trituration is taken to be the equivalent of one dilution in the centesimal scale. Once the substance has been rendered soluble, dilution can proceed in the normal way.

Index of Symptoms and Disorders